*an anthology of poetry
1975–2025*

JOHN ROBERT KEYSER

The Artist of Mesquites
Copyright © 2025 by John Robert Keyser

Published by Jester Entertainment, LLC.

All rights reserved. No part of this book may be reproduced, stored in a retrieval system, or transmitted in any form by any means—electronic, mechanical, photocopy, recording, or otherwise—without written permission of the author, except for brief quotations in printed reviews.

ISBN: 979-8-90053-001-7 (print)
ISBN: 979-8-90053-002-4 (ebook)

Cover photograph: Jeff Stovall
Cover and interior design: Sara Hook
Editorial direction: Shannon Keyser

Table of Contents

A Brief Introduction 1

The Bouquet 3

The Bouquet 4	The Fort Worth Courthouse 24
The Last Rhino 11	The Invisible Fan 28
October Wind 13	Untitled 29
The Undelivered Flowers 16	Dust 30
The "Colony" at Christmas 17	The Flight of Life 35
A Glint Against the Stone 18	Long Island's Girl of the Sound 36
The Lawn Nymph 20	(As I Walk Down to) Sixth and Main 37
Flowers (Early) 22	In Tune with My Heart 39

Long Island Breathes 41

Long Island Breathes 42	A Distant Speck of Light 57
Shells 45	Flight 800 59
The Dance of Color 46	The Young Soldier's Grave 60
God's Scripted Name 51	A Monument to 9/11 62
Island Cabin 52	(Save) New England's Open Space 63
Poet Laureate of Aquebogue 54	The Last Leaf 66

Ghost Ranch 67

Range of Ghost Mesquites 68	Shadows 80
Hallways 75	Century Plant 81
Sight 77	A Place Held Dear 82
A Lone Star State of Mind 78	The Artist of Mesquites 84

Upward Unto Mountain Pathways ... 85

A Seed Once Planted ... 86	Environmental ... 99
Black Bear ... 88	The Appalachian Trail ... 100
(A Conversation Between)	Mountain Goat ... 102
An "Old Man" and the "Upstart" ... 89	Gratitude, "TToo" Begins with "T" ... 104
Armadas ... 91	Hills ... 106
Mountain Bluebird ... 92	Imaged Mount McKinley ... 107
Keyser, West V.A. ... 93	Halo-cloud ... 108
Falling ... 94	Mountain Echoes ... 109
Wolf Creek Pass ... 95	Upward ... 110
Streetside ... 96	

The USA in Verse ... 113

What Is a Song? ... 114	Tornado! ... 135
Poetic Diversity ~ Essence of Our Land ... 115	So Early and So Late ... 136
Patriot ... 128	America, the Changing ... 138
Highway View ... 129	Hurricane ... 142
Our Flag ... 130	Return Home ... 143
Mosaic of States ... 131	The Lunar Date with U.S.A. ... 144
Exchange ... 132	Reunion ... 145
Secret Place ... 133	The Millennium Stone ... 146
Citizens ... 134	The Fabric of Our Flag ... 148

Our World ... 151

World of the Mind ... 152	Weeping Glacier ... 166
Sameness ... 158	The Time Has Come ... 167
The Instant ... 159	Genealogy ... 168
Rainbow ... 160	Philosophy ... 169
The Perfect Language ... 161	Compassion ... 170
Nameless Intermittent Stream ... 162	Geography ... 171
(Ordinary Street Lamp) Of Kinship ... 164	A Poem for Success ... 172
(A Necklace of the) Nations of the Earth ... 165	The Whirlaway Waltz ... 173

Space 175

(The First) Night Launch	176	"The True Super Bowl"	192
A Planet's Title	187	The Heavens	198
Transcending	188	Space Knowledge	199
Space Interrogative	189	Life Star	200
Alone	190	My God is Proved Within Itself	201
Infinity	191	The Concept of Love	202

Additional Works 209

The Golden Key	210	The Random Stone (Named "Hildegard")	211

About the Author 213

A Brief Introduction

This book is a compilation of my poetry collections, written over the course of years, sometimes in conjunction with other works of art or creative endeavors I was pursuing at the time. For me, poetry is a verbalization of emotion, and each of these books aims to capture those emotions. Below are summaries as to why each collection was written.

The Bouquet is my first and only book of love poems. It contains the emotion of love in sixteen poems—enough for a bouquet.

Long Island Breathes is a tribute to Long Island, my home for more than forty years. I moved to Long Island after graduating from college, and my wife joined me when we married a year later. This set of poems personifies many old memories.

Ghost Ranch includes the poem "The Artist of Mesquites" and is my marquee at exhibits. I was born and raised in West Texas and was surrounded by mesquite trees. This series of poems is nostalgic, remembering and feeling melancholy for the past.

Upward Unto Mountain Pathways was inspired by the years of retirement we spent in the Great Smoky Mountains of Tennessee, as well as some of my early college years in Colorado. With universal geographical areas, these poems deal with mountains and the ideas and feelings mountains bring to mind, such as loftiness, awe, holiness, and reaching up into heaven.

USA in Verse references historical points of interest in the United States. These poems contain varying emotions, from patriotism to tragedy to optimism.

Our World is a collection of poems centered around more abstract concepts and emotions, covering subjects like philosophy, time, and connection. There is nothing like the world of the mind.

Space contains poems meant to express wonder, to question if we are alone in the universe. It is paired with a piece of art called "In the Cosmos," which is a pointillistic painting made up of thousands of paint dots meant to emphasize our minuteness in a vast cosmos.

In addition to these poetry collections, I have also written two poems exclusive to this anthology.

"The Golden Key" is one of my more recent poems and was written to reflect on God's gift of grace as "the golden key." It is meant to convey a sense of hope and a theme of thankfulness.

"The Random Stone (Named Hildegarde)" is another standalone poem. I imagined, in my mind, finding a rock. I have a few random stones in my studio, and those stones remind me of the Rock of Ages—Jesus—which conveys the concept of Truth. This poem is one of confidence.

The Bouquet...
of sixteen poems chosen for you...

J. Keyser

The Bouquet

Rising . . .
Before the dew of night
Which kissed the sleeping petals
Awakens them by
The absence of its touch . . .

I set about to gather
Poetry from life's
Field of flowers
Into your hand and . . .
The vase of your heart.

And the gift of dawn approaches
Adorned in somber blue-gray robes
Emerging from darkened pathos
Then slowly into splendor . . .

The beauty of Baby Day
Cradled in the aging arms of Earth
Is the gift I hand to you
As the midwife of this poem.

But how can I impart with verse
That birth of color . . .
Sunrise . . .
Whose rapturous hues bespeak
The silent gift of God?

Soon daylight will become
The herald of a million gifts
Of loving sight and sound and touch.
So, I give to you the gift of truth
~ that sacred illumination ~
From the blessed light of day . . .

I'll choose for your bouquet the sunburst
Which lights its million spheres

And each flower with its special radiance . . .
Light that fills a void within your heart,
Light from the tenderness of my hand
Through both touch and written word . . .

And each type of flower becomes a sonnet,
No one more beautiful in its way
Or more unique than all the rest.
Each has its part to play, it seems,
Its void of love to fill,
In this mood that we call life.

One flower will say "hello" in passing,
A little flirt by sight or scent,
And yet another will come forth
To brashly say "I love you"
In a way
That all the great poets of all time,
Made into one,
Could never quite convey.

I pick this flower for you, dear heart,
To be placed at center stage
And hope its tones and shape will finally speak
Those words which falter on my lips.

Each type of plant, pulled by the sun
From a nurturing soil . . . from that miracle of life
Among the planets that we call earth . . .
Such botanical growth at some point
Near the dawning of its age,
Will have produced that sapling
Rising with the mist of earth and time
Into a noble tree . . .
Into the largest and oldest of living things.
And so,
I choose to include it now
As my love's emblem of enduring strength.

And what other shall I include in your bouquet, love,
The budding trees and shrubs of spring
Or a blush of autumn leaves,
those floral sprays of nature's giants
Covering mountain sides and dales?
Then, oh, the banks of verdant green . . .
Banks of foliage ~
Lushness for your eyes and heart.

Yet let us not forget such smaller plants
As lacy ferns on valley floors.
These shall edge my vase of love
With repose and delicacy.

And even in the season's sigh of death
Beneath a grave blanket of winter snow
Bedecked by holly berry and evergreen
My love that lingers . . . though petals fade . . .

Touch with me, now, each form of life,
Each with its dance and movement
Within its solitary journey
~ electrifying ~
No matter how long or short its stay.
Could not the romance of
Such a dance be captured
. . . to, in turn, captivate your heart . . .
Somewhere within the bouquet
That I have picked for you?

Of all zoological treasures lost
I can least imagine
A sky uncut forever
By wondrous, feathered wing.
Oh love, I then must include
Within your most treasured vase
Their plumage of a thousand hues

And let your heart soar on vibrant wing
With each dream that you hold dear.

These birds within their vaulted world,
Alone to savor the endless blue
And glide toward the virgin clouds
Which change always in majestic shape
Sculptured as by God's own hand . . .
I give them flight within your heart
With every prayer I breathe.

And leafy cathedrals have become their homes
Where it seems that they, like angels,
Refuse to be earthbound
~ And upon a whim ~
Mount even from those treasured heights
Toward the unbounded blue of heaven.
That home within unfettered heart
I leave for your abiding place.

Unmatched in nature, too, arise
Their spring and summer songs.
Within every warbler's rhapsody,
The sound of life and love, of joy and hope,
Adds light unto the day.
And their songs seem yet to linger
Into the dead of night.

Those notes carried by wistful breeze
Wafting upon the chords
Of nature's orchestra
Render all life more thrilling
Than ballads made for kings.
Can't you hear them too?
Let their notes now and forever rise
As with gilded wings
Into the roofless chambers of your heart.

And what of their reflected sky
In ocean, lake and pond
If not a sign of heaven here beneath?
The throbbing heartbeat of this earth,
The sea,
Pulsating life with its lifting tide
. . . surging swells and waves within its breast . . .

The oceans bringing forth life in every form ~
Mist rising back into the boundless blue,
Into clouds from whence our life blood comes,
Pouring rain into the veins and arteries of life
~ river, stream and brook . . .

And as the course of life forever flows
Back again into heaven's blue,
I wish eternal life to fill your soul.
And if your surge of love's for me
. . . Or someone else . . .
May, also, that flow eternal be.

So I lay back, resting now, and
Look into the sky
From whence comes the deeper
Life-giving blue of earth.

And nearby, the whispering stream
Forever speaks of life within its flow.
Wayside ponds and lakes
Receive that blood of earth,
Each into its cresting breast.

Azure canopies of distant seas
Conceal a mystic world beyond our own,
A place where shafts of light sometimes betray
An Eden where exotic shapes and floral growth
Cover majestic hills and valley floors, explored,
Only by the magic shapes of neon fish,
A place where reality and myth

Mix together in blue and green.
These shells and coral palaces
I leave to you alone
as your place of sacred dreams.

And now I bequeath unto you
From all the animal life on earth
Virtues of wisdom, grace and speed
Of power and timidity
Clothed in sometimes glorious robes.
And all of their domestic counterparts
Along with butterflies and bees
Have brought such wonder to our lives!

From mammoth to the microscopic . . .
From amphibious to the desert ant . . .
From other planets where life may be
Viewed through telescopic means,
To the wonder of a cell beneath another lens.
With such astounding things,

I place that sense of wonder in your hands
So the thrill of life will remain
Each time your eyes behold another dawn.
And what of mankind, now
~ The polished stone of life ~
Who mined the jewels and golden crown
Which I place, too, within your hand.

Who fashioned the victor's laurel wreath
Who conquered land and sea and space
Who wrote love's song,
All of which I pass as with
A single volume unto you
Bound with a heart-shaped clasp.

But most importantly, a crown of thorns,
Of service, love and care,
A crown of self sacrifice which

Only you can fashion in this world
~ a crown ~
To be touched only by angelic hands
And placed before the throne of God.

And, finally sunset . . .
Isn't it something
What God can do with color?
. . . Beautiful, even as the death of day
Precedes the glorious night.
Beautiful as I put its flower
Colored with angelic hues
At last into its place.

I bequeath, now, these random bits of verse
With all my care into your hand.
I know it's not a lot
. . . just a snippet gathered here and there . . .
As I knelt down upon
My valley floor for words.
I may not have chosen well,
But I took each flower of this bouquet
Tenderly from my field of love.
I picked them for you . . .

The Last Rhino

It is noon. Yet, for the rhino,
Sunset's last, red flaming ball
Has rolled out into his dusty world.

He has never needed stealth
In the power of his approach.
Can't you hear them now . . .
The thundering footfalls of the last rhino?
Can't you feel the shaking earth
As he rattles the bass strings of nature?

Then abruptly he stops.
Not because of fear ~
(His genes are too strong to know
The meaning of such.)
But to listen, to sense, and gauge ~

Weak little pig eyes stare fearlessly
As they strain to measure his foe through the dust.
With latent power,
He mocks the world with his horn.

Even in infancy, he was never small
. . . just a baby bulldozer
Complete with the arrogance
That goes with being such.

Too powerful and unaware to be afraid
Of the devices woven around him by modem man,
He steadily lowers his menacing horn
Straining to ascertain the poacher's dim image.

The hunter aims his rifle and, at that point,
Becomes less than his victim.
The last rhino will die there amid the rocks
Without knowing the meaning of compromise.

With the lumbering power of controlled chaos,
Amid the shaking earth and clouds of dust,
He pile drives straight ahead
. . . into the past.

Nature's violin and piccolo will still be there
. . . at least for a while.
But what of the tuba and bass drum?
There, within the red sunset,
A virtuoso lies dead.

October Wind

Strange winds rush about
The darkened autumn woods.
Leaves and twigs rise up
Alive yet dead.
The wind becomes their souls
. . . but hideous ones they are,
These forms which whisper
And sometimes howl.

The wind's alive . . . or is it?
Yes . . .
Something's alive and moves
Within the once still wood.
Icy fingers from winter's death
Probe with gusts
Which threaten first
Then tear the leaves of spring
From once pleasant maple trees.
And sometimes they reach
Cold fingers through winter cloaks
Into fearful hearts.

I bring alive the dead,
Coarse wind that I am.
Do you hear the creaking
Of long dead barnyard doors?
That is the voice I take.
Why tremble you at
The shutter's wake?
It lies so still until I
Inhabit it with a slamming siege.
With a loud hammer
I bring back movement to that
Which once lay dead.

So it is with dead fears
Which once you buried
With fearful, sweaty palms.
My icy fingers now pry them loose
One by one,
Those heavy funeral stones,
Until the monster which I have loosed
Gains lodging and lives anew
Within your personality and mind.

You may scoff and say I don't exist
Until you meet me on some darkened country path
A hovering figure, scarcely shaped . . .
I'll let your horror complete my form.

You'll feel my breath
And perhaps a crackling laugh
As I draw forth your secret fears
Which give me life as a vampire's blood . . .
Which gives me the nature you shall possess
As I reflect the horror stored within you
Back to stare you in the face.

So you've "outgrown" me, eh?
Don't be too sure
Lest at some unknown hour
~ If you dare to walk within the darkened place ~
I will pounce upon you
As I did the once, dead rubble pile,
And swirl within your soul,
. . . that same wind that lately swept
Through the gravesites' ghoulish moor.
I will squeeze between the plankings of your mind
As through the boarded house on yonder hill.

Tonight I give legs
To all your goblins and various ghosts.
Hear them stirring in the nearby wood

Bathed in the orange moon glow?
I become the witch's cackle
Or the werewolf's howl.
Listen carefully.
Don't you hear me beyond
Your casement windows?
I become the life of all your fears
. . . I am the October wind.

The Undelivered Flowers

They stand now, cold within the florist's vault,
Golden captors of loving sunshine . . . waiting
To thrill some longing heart and bring
Rays of bursting brightness into a shadowed hour.

Blushing in that golden moment of their prime
They stand waiting in the lobby of a patron's heart,
Each with anticipation and with bated breath,
Each for its chance to say, "I love you"
With the fragrant beauty of an angel's touch.

But sometimes as moisture collects and rolls like tears
Down the inside of the viewing glass,
Their waiting place for love becomes an icy crypt.

And as the petals wilt, perhaps unopened,
They will be cast into a bin
Where dreams, unexpressed, have gone before.
Lost now ~ the moment of their golden glory ~
Lost ~ the chance to warm another's heart ~
I see them fading there . . . waiting rays of sunshine . . .
Those flowers which were never sent.

The "Colony" at Christmas

It may be
That a crest of fallen snow
Covers the meager habitat
Of brier and bush
Or perhaps not even that.
Maybe just the blister
Of cold winter wind
Penetrates the lair of homeless cats . . .

Crouched in forms of yellow, white and black
Huddled perhaps in groups of two or three
Looking out into a world which
They cannot befriend
And one
Which has not befriended them.

A Glint Against the Stone

Within the starlit shining night
My car ride became a floating dream,
The thrill of achievement and
Anticipation of a new tomorrow
Coursing with happiness
Through my veins and joyous mind.

Then, in a quickly forgotten flash,
My lights caused just a reflected glint
Off some stone within the silent garden.
I'll never know which one,
Though I might search in futile quest.
Nor would the person buried before it
Realize the instant caught.

Just a tiny flash
~ that's all ~
From the headlights of my car.
I would no sooner pause to ponder
That dark burial ground just now
Than I would the movement of engine parts
Beneath my hood.

My drive continues as would a buoyant dance,
A waltz across the stage of life,
And each form upon which my headlights fall
Becomes an embellishment to life's cheerful day.

Why, then, should I stop to pry
Into that brief instant
So unconnected to the thrill of life?

What contrast it makes
Dark and alone within the jubilant night.
The lifeless eyes of markers stare
At somber trees and shrubs which also

Witness, by day, the silent host.
There only moon and stars belong,
Casting dim light upon a changeless scene.

Some forgotten stones stand fading
Flake by flake
Stones which have not for ages seen
Tear-stained cheeks or anything
More than blown leaves across their wakes.
Nothing new merits notice in that field
Where change has forever ceased.

The fleeting instant thus has passed
Along with its tiny glint
Almost unnoticed and barely seen.
The yard lies silent still
And calls out, but in a way unheard,
As my car lights continue to shine across
A million scenes of jubilance
Exciting . . . full of hope and living joy.

The Lawn Nymph

I don't remember where or when
But I recall the cloudy, rain-stained day
And wisteria clinging to aged mansion walls
Or maybe there was no mansion nearby at all,
Perhaps just ancient, ill-kept vines,
Strangling scenes of former grandeur
With, it seems, almost an apology.

Her image, carved into the eternal youth of stone,
Remained standing, hardly noticed there,
Amid greater forms of aging glory
Which she was meant simply to embellish.

But I'm sure that, long ago,
The artisan had hoped her tiny form
And the gesture felt and carved
With such loving care into that rock
Might transfer the essence of her beauty
Into the aesthetic hearts of those beholding . . .
For, perchance, just one short, enchanted span.

And I cast but a single, fleeting glance upon
That youthful, captive smile,
Carved once quickly but for all time
Within a single, inspired hour,
Whimsical, alluring and always fresh
Never altering, even once, in tempestuous quest
As she looks at me alone ~
Yet also upon generations past and those to come.

The darkness of a thousand nights has passed
When moonbeams and starlight alone
Have played upon her mystic lips.
Still, she waits with tireless expectation
. . . never transposing even once in empathy
With raging storms or cold.

And when, perhaps, some generation yet to come
May crush that statue into bits,
The enchantment which once was hers
Will remain even within the rubble
Forever calling
Still, somehow, unchanged.

Flowers (Early)

The most delicate flowers start to sense
The icy taste of gall
And wilt their leafy arms before
The poison breath of fall.

Lilies bow their withered heads
And start to fade away.
The strongest roses finally drop
Their petals to the clay.

Gusty winds and killing frost
Now have conquered all.
Sleet and ice have killed their prey
And so the grave of snow can fall.

All is silent here . . .
The victory finally won.
The skies of gray have veiled the earth
And darkened out the sun.

The earth is cold and gray and bare.
Frozen stands the icy brook.
Through the months, each living thing
Toward a warmer season looks.

Though still dark and frigid, the geese begin
To wing their northern route.
From an eager sycamore
Some leaves begin to shoot.

Winter eve is over now.
Storm clouds from the waters rise.
Songbirds, from their leafy homes,
Burst into the open skies.

The flowering guests of spring now dot
The fertile, sunny ridge

Burst upon the mountain side,
And lily pads beneath the bridge.

They spray into the meadow grass
And creep along the valley floor,
Dance upon the moonlit hill,
And finally reach the lakeside shore,

Bloom along the sidewalk paths
And spring into city parks.
Flowers . . . red, blue, and yellow,
That steal into lonely hearts!

The Fort Worth Courthouse

Who would've thought it
After all these years
My still standing here
Unique and proud
Amid these structural whippersnappers?!

Some of them put together by computers
H-U-M-P-H!
Give me back those *real* builders
With their handsaws and such.
Instills a little pride in me, y'know.

A-W-W quit pawing over me.
I'm not dead yet!
I took care of myself before you were born
. . . O-O-PS!
Well . . . a crack here and there.

QUIT STARING, you modern buildings!
We'll see what YOU look like in 100 years!
You may not even be here then.

On second thought, I guess you will.
But look at all that help we gave you starting out,
The new technical baby formulas and all.

Don't get me started
Talkin' about that last tornado . . .
I can see those modern buildings now,
Their glass and parts scattered
All over the streets and sidewalks.
They're still cutting their eyes over
In my direction and whispering to one another,
"Looks like the old battle-ax
Has pulled through another one!"

All of this as I just stand proudly and unaffected
On the grand summit overlooking my domain.
By gum, I wish they'd quit saying,
"Just think of the stir she used to make."
There's still a couple of perks left in the old gal!
O.K., O.K., I've had a face-lift or two.
(Straighten those stones out a little over to my
Left, please. Thanks.)

As I was Saying . . .
What was it? . . . oh, yes,
I used to be admired
For the architectural marvel that I was
Intrinsically.
I remember them saying,
"Wow, look at that!"
As they gazed in wonder upon my
Powerful frame.
I was "top dog" in my day, Yessir!
Still command my fair share of glances.

Why, families used to travel for miles
Just to behold my prowess.
Cowboys stood right over there,
Chewing their tobacco and admiring me.
They came driving their cattle across
The Trinity River down there,
Which I have been staring at for all these years.
And I can remember the veterans of the
Two Big Ones marching up that street
And . . . oh well, I guess you're bored
At hearing us old folks going on and on.

Now I'm looked upon as much
As for what I USED to be
As for what I AM . . .
I'd trade a little reverence for some admiration

. . . but . . .
I guess I don't have a choice . . . do I?

They're always bathing me as if I can't
Take care of myself like these new buildings
Are capable of doing,
A little dehumanizing, I'd say.
How about a little respect? O.K.?
Remember those babies I started in this world
Through those marriage papers?
Yep, they came to ME.

But now all of my great power
Has been reduced to a spectacle
As I stand here all "gussied up"
Ready to meet the next hundred years or so.

That young "plastic surgeon" did such a great job
With his sandblaster.
And those new miracle paints and cosmetics
Have done wonders for my wrinkles.

Why just the other day a person said,
"Look how pretty!"
But, a-w-w, I think he was
Just saying that.

I'm a little worried about next year . . .
Major operation . . . the foundation, y'know . . .
A little touchy. Some don't make it
But I think I'll pull through again.
They're coming up with something new every
Year.

Instead of being senile,
I guess I'd better count my blessings.
My contemporaries . . . most of them . . .
Gone, dead and largely forgotten.

I'd better consider myself lucky
To be getting out with my hide!
Think I'll stick around
Just to see what happens next . . .

The Invisible Fan

The Little League player took his last swing.
He has missed every ball. They've lost every game.
The rickety stands contain only a few . . .
There is gloom in the air and the season is through.
But wait, the fan that matters is now on his feet
Yelling and clapping for that Little League team!
This unseen fan, the Lord up above,
Has watched every game and seen every move.
He's heard the coach tell the team to do right
While trying to win with all of their might.
Masters of the game left the field that day.
In the contest of life, they're now ready to play.

A major league player now steps to the plate.
The stadium is full, the fans breathlessly wait.
With his winning hit, the crowd jumps to their feet
But the unseen fan remains in His seat.
With head bowed low, He's seen the real man,
Who was missed by the coach and ignored by the fan.
While cursing and swearing and engaging in strife,
He has made a joke of God's rule book of life.
Though he's gained all the skills and with it the fame,
This man, as of yet, has not mastered the game!

Untitled

Now . . .
There is but the dust of dreams
Broken . . .
By dawn's cruel light.

Dust

The Eternal Instant whirls as dust
Without beginning and without end,
The last of its trailing haze
Not set apart against the first.
    And I see as air
    No . . . thinner than such
    An ageless concept within its twin emptiness of space,
    Forcing birth – the ensuing dust of matter –
    In a way not reckoned
    By art, philosophy or of science.
Ah-h-h, but perhaps the poet,
Always, today, underpaid and unrenowned
Through words, also, as dust adrift
Within the paths of air shall lead, at last,
Man to both the source and timeless throne of God.
    Thus, the ageless meanings of cloistered words
    Have always formed eternal concepts
    Invisible in perpetuity
    And a first concept in God's Holy Book
    Deceit
    Forever begging resolution
    Which could never happen within its
    Non-solid concept, absent change.
So that birth – first of dust – then of man
Started
With the mandate for resolution
Of the conflict within that single term . . .
Deceit
    And the *instrument* of its division comes
    From another mandated/eternal
    Concept: A necessitated
    Governing and restrictive "Holy Spirit" force.
    Oh this invisible power sensed –
    Innate within the term, deceit –

    Unrequited writhing demanding change
    And resolution, impossible in its
    Eternal given state of formlessness ~
    And therefore changeless ~ concept.
    So from the agitation
    Innate within the concept, deceit ~
    The birth-mother of causation ~
    Came a type of friction
    Pulling the, at first, unformed words
    "Let there be light"
    From an also mandated,
    Governing/Restrictive Force, divine,
    An illumination of sorts.
Thus, the Good Book of John also says
At its poetic start
"In the beginning was the Word"
        and
"In Him was life;
And the life was the light of men . . ."
Illumination . . .
That mandated start of separation.
    And so I see illumination
    As a form ~ and yet not really as a form ~
    Rather
    Like transparent, never ending "dust of time,"
    Necessitated and emitting from
    That eternal word/concept, deceit . . .
Since deceit cannot deceive itself
Into something it already is,
A creation of its divisional imperative ~
"Matter" ~ the entity which time can affect,
Compelled that "dust" of illumination,
Agitating,
As with the churn of birth pangs
At last into a directed movement;
A path of sorts . . . a whirl of iridescence
Still, yet, like some form of "non-solid dust."

So illumination, at first in a figurative sense,
Turned itself, like the inside of a coat,
Into, also, non-material light.
But the separative agent man
Had not yet appeared
To choose, as the necessitated
Divisional imperative
Between that light and dark.
Also two transparent poles of natural law,
Positive and Negative: Good and Evil
Ordained as necessitated by the Spirit force
Pulling toward resolution of deceit,
At first, futilely, in changeless,
Non-solid, conceptual form.
    Then compulsory, penetrating light conjured
    Expelling something akin to friction,
    Formless
    And yet, somehow a form
    Swirling like disintegrated dust also
    Into all areas where light illuminates
    In its peculiar shapes
And since the start, by its nature,
Is changed from nothing
Gravitating toward its natural, manifest end
From the swirl of agitational light
Into a yet non-material type of friction
Finally into energy
Swirling, always whirling into, at first,
A yet non-solid gaseous state
Before the dust . . .
Always churning toward the divisional imperative
Man . . .
The separation of deceit into its
Opposites ~ good and evil or
Truth and error ~ whichever one prefers.
    Thus within some point inside that circle
    Of falsely so called time

Which has no beginning – nor, therefore, end,
An eternal though invisible concept,
Sometimes robed with a word, "Deceit"
Retaining an intrinsic tension within that term
Cries to be alleviated
Through a most perfect divisional act.
And with it an also eternal concept
Of causation which may be termed, spirit "Will"
Which we term "Divine" because it is the fixed control
Of all natural – or eternal – law and concept
Which acts upon deceit
Toward its divisional imperative
Which we call man
And the eternal, divisional choices
Which we, of necessity and by nature,
Are compelled to make . . .
And how far does that dust of matter
– Planets and assorted other bodies –
Travel and extend into timeless space?
Only as far as man's telescopic means
Will ever see or sense
Within this divisional crucible
That we term "cosmos"
Because
Beyond that there is no need
Nor – therefore – cause/existence
If you can tell me, then, O poet,
In some few lines of crafted verse,
How non-material thought can proceed
From the solid gray matter
Of man's material brain
Then I will use the reverse to show you
How a non-material, eternal "thought"
Projecting matter into being
Comes from eternal "will power," concept/thought
And a non-material Holy Spirit train.
Thus, a path always leads two ways,

Theorist and philosopher,
That no one can deny.
    I therefore see a type of "dust-thought"
    Emitted from the
    Non-solid, concept, state,
      Churning, flowing and eventually forming
      Toward its destined end
Having manifested itself into man
As the ultimate divisional quantity
Through selective thought
And free-will agency.
    And as the dust of cosmos
    And of man . . .
      Came forth from nothing
      Or the special realm
      So it shall return
      Swirling and flowing back toward
      A fiery end of "time" which
        Was, again, but the first . . . beginning point.
Thus the division into separate, eternal parts
one of darkness . . . another light
One of heaven . . . one of hell
One of truth . . . one of error
Will have been – at once as always – and now complete.

The Flight of Life

If by chance a butterfly
Lights upon your arm
Within some special day of spring,
Amid the scent of flowers
And of misty pine,

Take time not to move
Nor resist the light intrusion
But, for the moment, cast aside
Rushful cares
And perceive with awe, instead,
The wonder of its wings.

For soon it will be gone
With all its beauty
Back into the breeze,
Drifting from place to place
Then out of sight forever
On wings of random flight.

Take time, now, for those you love
~ The priceless moment shared ~
Wafting in the breeze of time
And let them touch your arm.
The beauty of their eyes and thoughts
Will not stay with you long
For soon
The cherished moment will take wing
Drifting, first, from place to place
Then out of sight forever
On wings of random flight.

Long Island's Girl of the Sound

Lithe and supple as her Island home,
She walks tall within the maple's shade.
History and nostalgia come quietly to her now
As bare feet touch the crystal sand.

Rivers of light wind forth from city streets
And past her cliffs and summer fields.
Yet brown eyes see only foam-crest waves . . .
She's the Long Island's girl of the Sound.

(As I Walk Down to) Sixth and Main

Both time and shadows lengthen now
As I walk past familiar city streets
Past the high school, Polish Town and railroad yards
And all the places in between.
Visages of youth and present happiness
Mark those scenes so long held dear
And yet, I see within the distance
The rest home's dark, impending spires
But scarcely noticed out the corner of my eye
(and that, perhaps intentionally so)
As I walk toward my future abiding place
. . . Down to Sixth and Main.

There dying hopes and dreams, it seems
Match its somber robes of flesh . . .
Melancholy shadows slowly moving
Leaving shadows of the past
For a shadowland of hope.

That building looms within a place
Where the doors swing inward only
And exits form in subtle, unknown ways.
Invitations and welcomes written
On gray recessive walls
Covered by whitewash
Or bright and cheerful hues . . .
Smiles worn on faces
Also adorned, sometimes, as masks
Await my arrival at time's last hour
. . . Down at the corner of Sixth and Main.

But now ~ just for a moment ~ I turn aside
And lose myself in the magic of the midday sun
Diversions built into the hour of youth
Serving to belie the truth and hour of age.

And perhaps such joy, at times,
Is accented all the more through contrast
With the image of that impending edifice
As I make my way down to Sixth and Main
And pick up trinkets from local shops
Which I shall possess but for a while.

Many times before – in shadowed dreams –
I've walked down that avenue
And buildings change, as sometimes
Do the streets and towns.
And the type of rest home changes too
Within imagined ends.

Each step's an hour, a year, an age.
And with more trepidation and appreciation now,
I take each careful stride
Toward a dimmed and darkened destiny
So long ignored by all.

That home awaits the two of us
Though you may not describe it such
And boulevards of change will mark
Both our paths . . . down to Sixth and Main.

In Tune with My Heart

If I were to write, this hour,
A last bouquet of words to you,
I would include a song within the mix,
A song to match
The surging melody of your being
Pulsating
As with eternal, crested waves
Through the jaded temple of my heart ~
Our life blood awash somewhere within
The sound of that haunting back draft
Which courses through both mind and soul.

And as heartbeats spell, softly, out our song,
I become drunk with the sound of your name
And binge on the flow of your voice.
Your smile is an encore of joy
As our laughter echoes with one refrain
And lips that shape the sound of my name
Seem to embrace
With a single, rapturous chord.

I sense your presence always
Throbbing . . . forever coursing
Beneath life's sometimes
Crashing and erratic sea,
Matching my own heartbeat in waltz time,
Each rhythm a part of my own.

Strange, how two hearts become one stanza's part
With each ensuing breath and thought.
And I know that with the magic of each beat
Riding the high notes of nature,
Your life is a song played for me, love . . .
A song in tune with my heart.

Long Island Breathes

One dozen poems relating to Long Island and the Northeast

John R. Keyser

Long Island Breathes

Long Island seems to breathe with matching earthen lungs ~
Each expanding and contracting by surrounding ocean tide.
Those twin lungs, now and always filled with teeming life,
Pulsate still within
The throbbing rise and fall of ocean, bay and sound.

Lovely, always wafting, too, that island seems ~
Prone upon her glistening, sun-lit couch of sea
Inhaling and exhaling forever with
The force of its eternal tide.

I see her wake refreshed at dawn
From mist-blown sheets of crested wave
And rising, then, with matchless sunrise,
She travels on a highway by that name
Or moves somewhat westward by commuter train
. . . All dressed up like a fancy lady going somewhere . . .
And, bedecked with necklaced sea shells,
She struts toward Times Square
While retaining a little of her "country raisen."

Vapor trails and wakes of boats form ringlets
For her lovely hair and arms of commerce.
I see them waving ~ reaching upward, outward
Toward the world at large.
And seasons beckon from her glistening wardrobe ~
An array of multicolored styles summoned with the
Casual call, "What shall I wear today?"
She muses, "I've always looked great in blue."

Quite an interesting one with whom to converse, I'd say
~ a sense of history, art and science ~
And, over the years, she's entertained.
Schools, athletic fields and church spires
Beckon to her past yet seem to point ahead.

Statesmanship and politics become her and
She speaks to me of love ~
As building trades transform and sometimes reflect
The beauty of her nature.

She lends a hand to those less fortunate
And breathes a sigh of deep remorse
For tragedy and for crime
~ all in all, a good one to get to know.

Oh, she's a little fickle now and then . . .
A little unpredictable with those showers
Blowing off the Atlantic ~ with so little notice ~
And a first-class tantrum or so, as in '38, '57 and '85
. . . but such hurricanes are rare.
Beyond that, she seems next to Eden's garden
With a tempered clime and pleasant landscape
Where just about anything can grow.
"Doctors and beauticians," as it were, perform
With environmental zeal to preserve/protect
Those attributes within her unique realm . . .
That miniature, pinewood forest, for example,
Contrasting eastward near the Hamptons
With giant sequoias on the nation's western shore . . .

I feel her breath now and always
Fresh upon my cheek
And that air of which we both partake
Wafts from and o'er the pulse-tide of our home.

Oh Long Island's very breath of air ~ its breeze ~
Drawn through the rustling brush of life,
Expands and contracts as somehow does my own
~ Bringing life's oxygen to the corpuscles
Of both its living soul and mind.
Then carbon dioxide ~ thus transformed ~
Returns once more into its breast.

Oh Island trees of which I breathe . . .
And of foliage also taking root
Within the heart of earth . . .
I, thereby, become one with you
Pulsating within buried minerals and streams ~
A part of me thus lies so deep
Beneath your fertile, sandy loam.

At last, when the expansion of my chest and mind
Shall cease,
Yet the Island's breathing lungs
Will continue always to inhale with the rhythm
Of bygone, matching heart . . .

Shells

Shells
Glistening always upon
The wayside, sandy shore

Some
Bleached by sun
And broken

Others
Ornate in form and prized
With pristine, colored shale

All
Now empty as I hear
Their former echo from the deep

Each
I place upon my shelf
As a reminder

Reverenced
As I touch and see them
For what they are or might have been

Shells
Deep colored and unique
With a hint of bygone days

Somehow
They whisper and
Seem to become

Relics
Of our own spent lives
Washed upon the shores of time.

The Dance of Color

Since I first set eyes upon the Northeast corridor ~
The land I've made my home now forty years and more ~
Its never-ending, captive grasp has been to me
Color, oh the changing richness of its color . . .

It's tragic not to linger for a while and drink
Of each season's blessed cup of tea,
Overflowing yet never filling
Heart and mind with color . . .
Color . . . always moving . . .
With its swirling, ageless dance.

Oh, Maine woods once torched by nature's autumn
Now flooding downward in cascading streams
Of yellow, red and orange ~ with a sip of gold
To be provided, in due time,
By our nation's smallest state.
New Hampshire's white birch mountains
Contribute to the mix when comes their turn
As do Vermont's eternal pines of green.

And Massachusetts adds a touch of ivy
Which seems to cover walls
Of mansion, church and school.
Then, not to be outdone, Connecticut accepts
That fleeting crown of color in its course
Changing even small roadside bush
Into a radiance not yet beheld.
Then, unstopped by water's edge,
Colors leap to grace my island home.

Shimmering leaves by now have crowned
The heights of New York's mountains to the north
Which, at first, in still repose,
Lay quiet for all to see . . . motionless . . .

In breath-taking interlude.
Then a gentle breeze brings forth
The glorious dance of color
To stir both hearts and,
Oft times, wearied minds.

At last, Pennsylvania's lush green boughs
Give way - though somewhat grudgingly -
Before its lover's golden rush.
Then, too, New Jersey's verdant heart is won
As gardens go to sleep . . .

Thus, each season plays its rapturous song
Changing one yet to another
As within a symphony . . .
Oh how the fleeting blush of summer's rose
Once added fragrance to
Its blossom-spangled hour
- To Longwood Garden's changing scene -
Until the <u>Great</u> <u>Conductor's</u> <u>hand</u>
Transposed thousands of that floral host
With the thrill of autumn leaf.

And frost has long since laid upon
The most northerly of lands
When somewhere in southern Delaware
A crocus blossom first appears
And the dance of spring begins anew
- with beauty unsurpassed -
Again toward the north.

But even in the dead of winter's season
I turn my thoughts
To mounds of white where nature rests
And to frozen shapes of founts and glassy ponds.
. . . The snow of age now, downward, slowly drifts
Covering the lower parts of legs and feet
As I reflect back once more upon
A skating rink in Rockefeller Square -

Where multicolored poinsettias gaze
From frosted city windows
Upon the glistening tree.

Swirling forms upon that rink
Remind one of the art within
A ballet house not far removed ~
And how that act is reminiscent
Of one's life itself ~
Where all the brilliant seasons
Have become the skater's dance.

Strange how that routine portrays
One of season's change ~
And, as the throngs of people watch and cheer,
They, too, become a part . . .

The presentation begins as expectation
In the silent poise of winter's hold
For, in the moment of that statuette,
All breaths are held
As if God were saying to us all,
"Just wait for what I have in store for you . . .
The beauty and the ecstasy . . ."

Then from that latent wonder,
In the grace of its beginning,
I see a springtime flourish,
Blossomed fresh with white and pink.
And then, O God, the light-green bud!
. . . Unspeakable with matchless hope and thrill
As with the love for newborn child
. . . Once now ~ and only once ~ to view
The perfection of its start.
Thus nature's rapture with its music's now begun
. . . Colors ~ pale yet vibrant ~
In the sweetness of that early breath.

Next, the program's heart becomes our summer
With its colors rich and rare.
And we must all decide within our dance
Just when to translate with empathy.
Each turn, each leap, each spin we make
Shall be marked as to degree ~
As for beauty and for skill ~
And, oh, the audience may stand at times and cheer
Though your judge may not always agree . . .

The third movement ~ that of fall ~
Begins the climax of life's symphony,
Replete with its tartness ~ and sometimes ~
Bittersweet, the rush of color . . .
As if to place some crown of unique beauty
Upon each tree and life once lived.
Spin now and let your autumn word be sweet ~
A departing cry of crimson / gold
With perhaps apology.

In some ways that part's much like the first
Now, too, laid bare in finished state ~
A work of art ~ for good or ill
. . . Or a more likely mix of both.

Then comes the stolid, final pose
Frozen in climactic death
Forever to be seen and known of man . . .
And the profusion, last, of color . . .
Flowers strewn upon the ice
As once upon the tomb
While within our breast the impulse
To mourn, perhaps, and weep ~
Or to kiss, to laugh, and love.

Now lacing, one final time, my bladed shoes
I shall turn again unto the ice

To reflect upon life's celebration
. . . And skate the dance of color.

God's Scripted Name

Long Island's shape looks rather like
A little signature of God
Placed beneath our country's shoreline
After He had finished all . . .

Thus, God penned that earthen name, it seems,
With a certain style of nature's longhand
Shaped by ice and wind and sea,
Between guidelines of ocean, bay and sound.

Then as, perhaps, some type of afterthought,
He drew a line of sand
"with a type of flourish"
Beneath that crested name.

Island Cabin

I stepped outside my Island cabin into
The winter's frosted scene to hear
A message borne of hope renewed . . .
Whispered by the breath of falling snow
Gently into silent stillness.

And one could almost hear within that waiting time
Where wood was split by cold and ice
A cry ~ a yearning from human hearts
To start anew ~ to build ~
Upon some dream held dear,
Perhaps in youth
. . . Perhaps . . . so many years ago.

Soon winter flowers held inside
Like sometimes dormant love and hope
Will be placed amid the greening fields
And groves of human hearts.
Thus, take care with each transplanted flower
. . . Take care with skillful potters' hands . . .
To place within some sheltered dale
So it may somehow take root afresh
Within the soil of life.

My cabin journey across the ranch of hope's new dawn
Must then begin at springtime
~ that birth of seasons and morning of the year.
There, amid its voices and thousand forms of youth,
~ stretching out across a dawning landscape ~
Each plant, with its earthly struggle
Is framed within the elements
Of present, past and future clime.

Will you not kneel within that field at springtime
To help straighten some new plant
Bowed, perhaps, by careless fate . . .

That season is so short and will not wait
Because the future for each one is now.

At the noontime season of the year,
My summer path leads through a legacy of care
Where lives have grown into maturity.
May all who've seen cathedral pine
With its dark-coned seed.
Or the strength of life fulfilled
Within an acorn's oak
Bolt as mallards from the rangeland pond . . .
And rush as would a colt at early dawn . . .
There to begin once more ~ and dream ~
There to start afresh and build.

Each life, too, will have its autumn dusk
Where deeds of helping God and man
Reflect in gold, in red, and yellow-green . . .
Then I shall return once more at fall time
To light my Coleman lamp and fire . . .
My place ~ an Island cabin ~
Where each can also enter in
To dream and start anew.

Poet Laureate of Aquebogue

Oh little span of jeweled green
Unrenowned among the major townships of the world
Or, in fact, even among those tiny hamlets
Bordering one another along the length
Of Long Island's North Fork strand ~
Perhaps there's something we hold in common
. . . that being a lack of notoriety . . .
As housed in great centers to the West,
The North, The South and to the East ~
Across storied lands of splendor and of wealth . . .

Still how unique and joyful was that hour
When the title was bestowed on me,
"Poet Laureate of Aquebogue" ~
A citation from just the bare beginnings
Of a small town with its fledgling scribe.

Some may question how it's so . . .
Where no such proclamation was ever signed
And where not a single group or person
Can point to me and verify . . .

O.K., O.K., so it was a turtle.
I must admit ~
Not the most astute of citizenry!
And, I'll have to say, the circumstance
And place of confirmation
Was not the most esteemed and dignified . . .

It happened on a morning walk upward toward the sound
When I noticed a tiny hump upon the road
Which a car had narrowly swerved to miss.
Then, seeing an approaching truck and cars,
I ferried the turtle to the other side
His head yet tucked inside his shell.

Then slowly . . . cautiously . . .
His aged head emerged and spoke,
"Whew-w, that was another close one!"

"A talking turtle!" I exclaimed.
"Well," he responded, not slightly miffed,
"A dry-land tortoise, to be exact!
That crossing's always been a tough one for me
And I'm not known far and wide
As the NASCAR of Aquebogue!"

Then, with a change of tone, he spoke with pompous air,
"Because of your kind act, I shall endow you with
My final cabinet position to be filled.
With the power vested in me as the lord Mayor of Aquebogue . . ."
"Lord Mayor?!" I interrupted aloud
And continued almost by reflex, "Who appointed such?"
"Obviously you humans wouldn't understand," he snorted
Glaring at me with one red eye,
"Some deer, fox, rabbit and a squirrel
Not to mention my reptile base with its sizable vote
And a few absentee ballots from duck and geese . . ."

Then, with head hoisted high, he continued,
Still obviously perturbed by my skeptical remark,
"Nevertheless, for possibly saving my life,
I dub you 'Poet Laureate of Aquebogue.'
Of course," he continued with a humorous touch
~ tittering in his derisive way ~
"You're the *only* poet that I know of in my realm!

Sorry I can't offer you a certificate of recognition.
And as for that contemplative pond," he chortled
(concealing with one tiny foot
All but the corners of a smile),
"Yon sump hole must now suffice!

Unhand me now upon this field!" he then demanded,
Feet already gesturing as to walk.

For a while I watched him slowly
Traverse his kingdom step-by-step
Until the ground fog almost obscured
The tiny, caramel shape.
Then once ~ and only once ~ he turned his head
Backward to look at me
And with a look of amusement seemed to say
"Continue to write of our fair land . . ."
And, with that, we never met again
Though, within the fog, I sometimes wonder . . .

A Distant Speck of Light

. . . Just one of a million sets of auto lights
Flashing by on opposite lanes of I-495 . . .
And, not chancing more than peripheral view
It might have never meant to me
More than a single speck
Within that white river's endless flow.

The dash of light, in fact, became
Almost indistinguishable as an entity,
Merging into its millionth part of
All that lay before . . . beyond.
Yet even that small glimmer
Which added just slightly to the whole
Made it astounding in power of change
. . . of influence . . . profound . . .
Charged . . . a present mood now altered
~ no matter how small
Or insignificant it first appeared . . .
A tripping line of cause-and-effect
Leading as reactive chain
To matters so immense and small, the mind
Cannot contain it all.

And within that tiny glint of light
I've become a part of all that gleam will ever be
And from whence it came.
. . . inseparable . . .
In present, past and future time,
Representing and influenced by
Every contact ~ direct or indirect ~
From which that single beam has come.

I've, at once, become
And, therefore, have always been
A part of all of human life
Of which the origin

Of that light has ever touched
. . . all the birthing rooms,
Family picnics,
Joy and pain
We have forever shared
. . . Though unfathomed and forever unbeknown
Within each human psyche thus involved.

And my light viewed from the opposite lane
Would also change all who ever saw its glimmer
And bring my total self into *their* lives
Until a circle then is formed
Of eternal timelessness and involving all
. . . as spherical . . .
As that radiating glow from headlamps ~
From each tiny speck of light . . .

Flight 800

A pyramid of red, showering flame,
Framed within the early night
. . . how was I to know
What this sight was to become?

The emblematic burst meant little
Beyond a fiery question mark
To be lost perhaps amid spectacular equals
Within the crowded warehouse of memory.

But a light becomes an embellishment
Of that which gives it meaning
And soon the glowering scene
Explained with faces pressed against the heart.

I now see with each falling ember
A failing hope
And, as the cooling fragments plunge,
A darkened end to earthly loves.

To those like me who did not know them
(but, perhaps, somehow did within a brotherhood)
That flaming monument will always
Hang within the sky
~ and I will always see it there ~
A period at the end of life's stories
. . . a period at the end of dreams.

A curse, then, upon that flame
As it burns within my memory.
It will never eclipse a love glow from within
Nor the dazzling light of influence.

Emblazoned before my eyes as then
. . . but now with meaning,
I touched lives with them though shortly
And always it remains . . .

The Young Soldier's Grave

It escapes me, just now, why
~ amid the life and beauty
Of one sunlit, summer day ~
That I walked into a soldier's cross-strewn field
Where flowers languish in a last bouquet . . .

And, at random, paused before his marker
Not quite able to express
Just why I was standing there . . .
A stranger to both the name and
Two early dates, so very close in years.

Then ~ before a single word of homage
Came to the forefront of my mind ~
A rush of feelings tied to a thousand graves,
Through this symbol, spoke to me.

It was a paltry tribute, I'm aware . . .
That one brief tho sacred moment
Packed somewhere in among
The emblems of my superfluity . . .
Yet a type of unseen shrine of my emotions
Was erected in the stillness of my heart

. . . There are symbols of service branches
And sometimes, too, religious signs
Emblazoned upon the weathered stones
But that does not begin to tell
The full story of life and love
Cut short by war's cruel thrust . . .

I can barely hear, in the distance, now,
Sounds of commerce, life and joy
Within the air which he once breathed.
Fruited plants and fragrant flowers
Once, too, were his in life

And his eye caught the beauty of a
Bird in flight ~ as I've seen just now ~
Not far beyond his stone.

It seems the platform of
My brief and silent tribute
Would be a debt of gratitude.
Appreciation would form the walls
And a golden dome would reflect my guilt . . .
Why, it might easily have been me
~ instead of him ~
Lying there beneath the soil . . .
Within that youthful soldier's grave . . .

It makes, now, so little difference
In this ~ my form of tribute ~
Whether to hero, coward or in-between.
The fact that he no longer lived
~ instead of me ~
Brings me to stand in silent tribute
And also with deeply thankful heart . . .
In a type of ever paled indebtedness . . .

A Monument to 9\11

Powers felt within the human breast
Lift me above the settled dust
Borne by humankind
And help to raise a monument upon
That scene of sacrifice and shame.

It shall be a forum built upon
Failed ashes of coercion, hate and fear.
And there shall be released instead
By twin, uplifted arms and hands
This admonition to all within the world
~ for each in his peculiar way;

"Look inward, now, with minds so free to choose
~ from all religions, philosophies and paths.
The guiding light henceforth shall be
Research, reason and debate,
Yet not to be forgotten
The love for God and humankind."

And once this shrine is built within each heart,
I shall finally hear from breaths once lost in pain
A whispered sigh of rest;
"Go all now into your separate ways of peace."

(Save) New England's Open Space

How rare, the primeval, sacred view
Of nature's canvas all stretched out
Beneath New England's endless well of blue
A priceless work of art inspired
By breath of pond and ocean breeze
And painted only once
By nature's brush of happenstance.

I traverse that path laid out by fate ~ one
With as little managed help from man
. . . As possible . . .
Just to note the wild and unobstructed scene ~
A place where nature, at some unguarded moment,
Reveals her personality ~
An unspoiled portrait of herself,
Unrefined and not retouched ~ where
Hereditary genes are all apparent
With roots into her distant past.

Oh, I'm surprised how weak and timid
Nature now appears ~
The melancholy of the "tiger's eye"
Now caged and trained
When once it posed so great a threat.
Thus nature, for eons all pervasive
In the very essence of its global strength,
Seems at last to have succumbed
In a battle with its human part . . .

And if not careful, conquering man
Will come at last to spoil
The fount of his beginning and
Will come of late to realize
That the death of one's earthly habitat
Stills the heartbeat of his soul and spirit ~

To drain identity and with it meaning
From his very breath of life.

. . . No sounding board for man's advances
Nor anchor for the slingshot of his deeds . . .
No base of his beginnings with which
The meaning of this hour is kept!

And the song of New England's open space
Is a rhapsody of our old world,
Played anew each time that we behold.
And its strains of tranquility lace the heart,
Unmatched by orchestra or band
. . . A melody of birth
To soothe and re-create
The view of our beginning.
And an attempt to embellish its wild state
With the trappings of any man-made scene
Is as futile as to retouch a flower
Once completed by the hand of God!

Oh save that open space of land,
A jeweled piece, struck once divine
~ The unique, vast wilderness ~
Of nature's wild bouquet . . .
Leave always in its virgin state
To the trust of our posterity.

We must work alongside
And in cohabitation
~ man and nature ~
Each respectful of the other's role
~ kept apart as much as possible ~
Each to reign within its realm.

Let, then, sunrise and sunset forever rest amid
Its flowered plain, long stretched river valley
And sun-kissed mountain range.

I want, at times, to find my spirit lost within
Unfettered peace of forest growth or rangeland grass
- To stir again my quest for life
With the rustle of a woodland animal or bird
Caught by surprise at my intrusion.
- This my plea to save New England's open space -
Where, for old time's sake, I can return
To the land of its uncharted heart . . .

The Last Leaf

It was spoken of both good and ill
By winter's whispering wind . . .
The last leaf that lately fell
Within the farmer's sheltered dell.

I saw the leaf wave gamely
For days and weeks beyond its time . . .
A lemon yellow flag of sorts ~
Tinged here and there with bites of
Crimson lace around its fringe.

I hope that others, likewise, saw
With something more than just their eyes,
The patient battle that it waged . . .
This leaf that lately fell.

"GHOST RANCH"

FEATURING:
"RANGE OF GHOST MESQUITES"
AND SEVEN OTHER SELECTIONS

WRITTEN BY
John Robert Keyser

Range of Ghost Mesquites

Gray forms of ghost mesquites
Writhe and churn into the desert air
With uplifted, swirling body shapes and arms.
So like those of long lost spirits, they
Seem always wondering and grasping still,
With bony hands and thorn-sharp nails,
For some type of treasured, earthbound quest.

So much like spirits of other things about
~ In fact, so much akin they seem
To searching souls of those beholding . . .
Oh mesquites reflect the turmoil
Of my own life's twists, mistakes and turns ~
And with its thorns, so much the pain . . .

Thus when you see them after I have passed
Think of my spirit left within them too
. . . not of some powerful, straight and towering tree
But always repentant,
Touching earth yet pleading to the sky . . .

If you listen quietly and at certain times
You can almost hear a lonesome voice
Within the mesquite bean rattle
And a whispered message which
Only wind blown through
Its lovely, lacy leaves can make.

Oh such ghosts they call me back forever
And I imbue the beauty of what they are and were
With memories of wind blown through her winsome hair.

Those serene and beckoning arms and hands are
Given life by my beloved remembered breeze.
And I feel their call forever ~

Back to the land of my youth,
Back to **my range of dreams** . . .

Perhaps it's best that I write these words first in script
To match the flow of light mesquite tree limbs within
The Southwest's dry and storied air.
See how their tiny, shimmering leaves
Seem to speak into the breeze.
Seed pods only rustle slightly ~ perhaps almost unheard,
Adding subliminally
To that lonely, winsome voice . . .

Its whispered message speaks of times and people
Gone before . . .
And somehow of my own life's story
~ played out and personified within ~
Its long, stretched fibers . . . alive just now ~
Yet eternal somehow within
Life's never-ending instant.

Swirl on still, oh rangeland breeze . . .
Dip and dive with a whirlwind's gentle touch
To carve the features of earth's creviced face.

Oh, life-giving breath of breeze
Give me motion now to the mesquite tree's
Gently flowing arms and hands
Which reach into and form
The essence of my life and soul.

I shall take some time to rest a while
Beneath the ever-moving sparseness of its shade
And let its nostalgic voice speak once,
Yet always, of the scene stretched out before me ~
Of my Southwestern range and youth . . .

Gaze now with me upon
The beauty of nature's shorthand.

I plainly see the Southwest's soul within
Its barren red and yellow clay
Spotted here and there with restless spans
Of multicolored sand.
Rich earth seems, there, but a rarity
Too arid to produce.
And water, because of scarcity,
Becomes its jeweled case.

Haunting shapes that latch forever unto
Human souls, born into a desert's midst or
Journeying out its way, bedeck
The eternal, never ending landscape.
And forgive me if I wander in this verse
. . . because the mystic shapes . . . they
Seem to wander, always, too . . .

Dry weather preserves those ghostly forms
Beyond the days of those in damper clime . . .
I see skeletons of bygone wagon trains
Moving somehow still.
And man-made enterprises,
Long forgotten and cast aside, seem yet
To breathe . . .
Ghost forms of long-dead trees and
Other shapes of desert growth deceased
Appear yet to live . . . peculiarly . . .
Within dry and hollowed bodies ~
And eyes somehow seem to watch always
Through slits in long-dead wood.

Rangeland soil ~ that soul of earth ~
Seems, at times, to upward reach
In forms of naked stone, plateau and mountain peak,
As the unclothed forms which God hath made
Magnificent ~ adorned yet here and there
With the "fig leaf" of yucca plant, cactus shape or desert bush.

Oh how beautiful that colored stone by day
Reaching always upward to
A matchless sky of pallid blue
Adorned at times
With clouds which make one wonder of
God's creative touch
And hallowed shapes of things beyond.
Wondrous how those hillside colors match
Sunrise and sunset ~ eternal in their beauty too ~
As might brings forth its rest
For cactus flower and other wearied desert bloom
Strewn for so short a time upon
This arid yet intriguing
Skeleton of earth.

Speak to me, yet again, mesquite
Of your kindred trees. I see you point
Gray arms in your thousand ways toward
Isolated groves of live oak, so like, too,
The soul of man ~ alive and evergreen
Through brittle and never young they seem ~
Through every season and for all time . . .

Your withered arms point also t'ward
Rare stands of ageless cedar groves . . .
We shall let them be a semblance of
Some type of desert Christmas tree
In lieu of majestic northern fir.
Its aroma, too, with storied timelessness,
Is drawn into the lungs, the heart,
The mind . . . the memory and soul.

Here and there, as
Almost an intrusion, so it seems,
Abide the forms of, shall we say,
The more conventional of trees;
Pecan, tall cottonwood and willow, even

A stunted type of twisted oak
Take hold ~ almost in desperation it appears
In coves where the whispered promise, "water,"
Pulls them forth with sometimes short-lived hope.

So few binds of any type there
Seem to light upon
The mesquites' leather, outstretched palms
And the chaparral which run about its feet
And upon the rangeland floor
Seem hardly to be a bird at all
But an apparition ~ real yet somehow . . .
Not real at all . . .

And so much like that kindred spirit,
Jack rabbits, armadillos and horny toads
Breathe a peculiar type of life
Into that which oft seems dead.
And they yet perform some type of desert ritual
To keep alive the ghosts still there.

Oh how mesquite seed pods perpetuate
That never-ending image ~
Alive and always moving, so it seems,
Though still and quiet the air . . .
How that eternal motion, though none at all,
Forever beckons me . . .

As I start the trek of **my return**
I shall begin in old **Fort Worth** ~
A place where "The West Begins,"
Named for a man who was never there
Yet, in spirit, somehow was . . .

There, once dormant mesquite tree fibers
Invigorate again
The essence of my soul and being
As do the veins and arteries of life.

And the ghosts of old-time feelings
Revive and live, anew, within.

Oh, there let me once more wander
Through that mystic forest wonderland
Uncontrolled
Just as its random flow of branches
Spread in their creative way . . .

I shall set eyes again upon that school in
Western Texas where a spark for writing and of art
Was nurtured in some unique yet wondrous way.
There, beside dry, rocky creek bed, I will
Reunite with the spirit of my youth.

And I shall range a little farther north and east
Toward my early, Bryson, childhood home
Where gray and gesturing arms
Help me never to forget.

I then, perhaps, will travel westward
To a place called "Ghost Ranch" where
The artist, O'Keeffe, seemed to paint the Southwest's soul.
I once saw a photo of its grand plateau
Where spirits seem to rise along
Its rugged sides ~ upward toward the sky ~
And there, if I am ever come to visit,
Shall be dipped my own brush into both
The paint and storied air
To be named, not of myself, but by
The forces ranging 'bout me,
"The artist of mesquites."

And if skills could ever match
The abandon, grace, and eternal flow ~
The pain, yet beauty of its being ~
Then such a title
Could be aptly earned.

Mesquite, your thorns are ever there
To mar a perfect semblance
As was the imaged Rose of Sharon
To follow Jesus to the end.

At last a prayer for me
As I view those trees in parting
. . . for the thorns which I have pierced
Into the leafy, lovely hearts of some
. . . Oh, God . . . forgive . . .

Now, therewith, shall I rest once more beneath
The million parts of its perforated shade
And watch light shadows move just slightly
Within the rangeland breeze
~ with a periodic rustle ~
So much like a winsome shower . . .

And the mesquites' light, hair-like twigs,
With countless, tiny, slender leaves,
Grow into the thinning air ~ with no points of demarcation
Between the sky . . . and the hint of its reality . . .
Only spans of tinted, light green wash
Placed here and there within ~ and fading into ~
Its pale and arid sky . . .

Just so, my transition, too, shall come
From life into eternity . . .
Undernoted and hardly noticed
Amid the enterprises of mankind.
And my ranging search of life shall end
As the romance of
Those lost and rambling boughs . . .

Hallways

More ghosts live in hallways, and certainly more vividly
Than in any place I know.
Oh yes, it's true – at least to me.
Perhaps you may have noticed too . . .
Call them what you wish
Ghosts, memories of the past who wait to touch but can't . . . whatever.
Spirits of loved ones who have walked down various corridors
Seem to linger somehow forever in the "L" shaped voids . . .

You can almost see that special one,
Waiting in place – always and patiently.
See them standing there forever . . . a smile upon familiar face
Excited and waiting to tell you something new
Or perhaps just repeat in some slightly different way
A phrase or two of which you both are fond
. . . or to begin some current narrative
As you walk always – one beside the other?
Hear that faint echo? Can't you
Almost hear footsteps in the hall? . . .

That person may have died some time ago –
Or may now live many miles away.
It could even be that they have almost forgotten
That the hallways ever existed and remains there
Barely in the subconscious
. . . and to you it may seldom come to mind
But the ghosts of past have not forgotten, have they?
Just notice . . . if you walk, perchance, down that hall again,
Maybe years from now,
Memories, fresh, having never left,
Have never tired – never grown bored or out of sorts from waiting.
And the memories have faces – or impressions of expressions
. . . even if you don't remember names or number
You can always hear their voices, laughter
And their footfalls in the passageway.

Or perhaps some words of tragedy, or of pain, were spoken
In or near an entrance to that hallway . . .
Those live too and never die,
Casting a glowering shadow always,
Though unseen by others . . .
Words never dying . . . echoing always . . .
Within corridors of both your heart and mind.

Oh, I've wondered why they live forever there
And never dissipate though one may have tried
~ And even succeeded ~ to erase for just a span
Memories of the time and place.
Maybe, I've thought it's the feet ~ the gait personalized
Within each step ~ and I'm sure there's something to it . . .
Shoes remind so much of life. Oh take them from the closet quickly
When they have passed away or else the loss remains so real
. . . and real always shall be
The echo of those steps within your mind.

Doorways open from the hallways
To a thousand worlds,
But those steps return again ~ always ~
To the corridor . . .
Wait for me, love, in that narrow way.
For you know that I will always be there . . .
Perhaps not in reality . . . but certainly forever
~ We two in spirit ~
In a hall that knows no time
Or tenant
Except that one abiding always
Which gives past footsteps meaning
And
A type of life eternal . . .

Sight

Oh the crashing sound of silent death
Within a pitch-black miners' tomb . . .
I became one with all
Previously lost and doomed perchance
To a smothering fate.
Whether in cave or man-made shaft,
Empty, bottomless, the emotional plunge ~
Yet encased and choked
Within that grave's dark place.

Who can really understand ~ except those trapped ~
The longing for air, the sun, and wind
. . . Beloved scenes fleeting by in the memories of some . . .
Desire! How defined and real that word becomes
As desperation culminates and drives forth
All else from others' minds.
Then how priceless within encroaching death
Becomes the commodity of time and
The preciousness of hope which before
Had been little more than casual words . . .

Then, providentially, this once,
How glad the sound of pick
Or drill from far above . . .
The sound of human tidings!

And the shaft brought up life within it
As I stepped into the open space ~
Into rescue's speechless rapture ~
Oh, for the first time I was to see
The rosebud tree on younger hill,
The grass beneath my feet . . .
The smile upon
Your sunlit face and lips . . .

A Lone Star State of Mind

I hear that you're going to visit Texas soon
To see a friend you chanced to meet
And I must go along with you . . .
If only on the wings of dreams.

You will not feel the same as me
When the bordering land comes into view
Nor do I expect you to look beyond that line
And see much difference in the soil . . .

It's just not there ~ dramatic change
That may transfix the mind into a fable ~
That the land has somehow made the people
Different in ways or deeds
That have turned them t'ward either good or bad.

Rather you shall see a country that's not, perhaps,
Any more spectacular than the place which you call home
. . . Perhaps just a stand of Johnson grass
And that grasshopper on a crackling reed
May be no different than the one
Twenty feet beyond that point
. . . Into your other state.

Instead, just pause with me when first
We set foot upon that boundary's strand
And let thought take flight within the breeze
Or stillness of that common scene.
Then draw, once more, the air of youth into your lungs
. . . Into and through your mind and being.
Where your memory also brands with childlike awe
The freshness of a first touch . . .

When first a mother's loving, gentle hand
Was felt upon your brow.

When first you sensed the flower's breath
And beheld, with spellbound eyes, its form.

Oh, I hear that same earth groan now
For a native, wandering son . . .
Missing barefoot prints within her soil.
And I feel the pull of starlit nights
Always the same ~ because of her.

Great people and great things
Come from all ages, lands, and homes
So do not tax me with the worth of each.
It's simply because the mind and heart recall
That the confines of this plain, mapped space
. . . Called Texas . . .
Became the Mecca of my journey and my Shangri-la of life.

Shadows

Two shadows cast upon the wayside path . . .
I cannot help but to suppose, in symbol,
That they might follow our identities ~
Forever static in eternity . . .
To make those dormant come alive
Which have once and always been.

We would therefore be "shadows," so to speak,
Of our own conceptual counterparts ~
Types of once-played videos
Yet having always been wound and stayed beyond . . .
"Shadows" which have made our souls and beings come to life
Upon a stage forever set ~ in timelessness . . .

Century Plant

Barefoot on the earth, within the memory of youth,
We stand ~ my sister and I ~ before the century plant . . .
A curio set inside the hot, dry sand and clay
Of our grandmother's front yard in Bryson, Texas.

The thorn-bordered, broadleaf plant
Will live to be a hundred ~ so goes the ancient tale.
Then, sometimes within its last year's throe of death,
One resplendent, fragrant blossom
Will adorn the patient, barren form . . .

Oh, do not analyze or dismiss that mental wonderland
Between its myth and reality. For yet
The nostalgia of its spell lingers as a part
Of a childhood romance which once thrived undisturbed
And should, forever, be allowed to rest.

Though the fabled blossom we never were to see,
We yet dreamed of "someday" when
It would come to flower.
And now I realize that bloom would finally signify
The budding of eternal youth
. . . An enticement of sorts
T'ward a rapture not seen before
In all of life upon the earth.

We stood in awe ~ almost transfixed ~ before the plant
Not in reverence of that plant ~ or of nature ~
But of a force in all of its profundity
Which stood behind the making of everything
. . . An entity . . .
Too powerful and complex to ever fully understand.

A Place Held Dear

There converged, one day, within my heart
Two diverse yet providential paths
~ one an unkept place not of my choosing,
The other a track of destiny and time ~
Then and forever bonded
By the converting miracle of love . . .

It was not mine to choose the hour or day
~ And certainly not that littered place ~
Where the transforming act of fate
Was to touch its sacred wand
To memory's special, gilded roll.

Still, I guess, in the back part of that scene,
The same ugly culvert scars the ground ~
Unworthy till this day,
To have a name bestowed upon
Its random, intermittent course . . .

It was just a drain of sorts
Where tires, tin cans and Styrofoam,
Trashed by careless hands,
Lay sometimes half submerged within its murky bog
Or thrown about its crusted path beneath and unrelenting sun.

On day, a city's working crew,
As, perhaps, some type of afterthought,
Decreed that drainage ditch flow into ~ then forth from ~
Some concrete pipes, meant to direct, somehow,
The meandering, muddled, nameless stream.

And its hapless field, transversed
By railroad tracks, electric lines, and fenced-in city towers,
Seemed to resist with spots of tangled bush, wild rose and briar
And ~ where once stood a forest's growth ~
Lay bulldozed, chain sawed, piles of logs

Oh, city service crews would, from time-to-time,
Make gestures of cosmetic surgery upon
The uneven, ill-kept lot
~ a perfunctory mowing of the grass
And gathering of the worst of junk . . .

Still, concrete spills and piles of rock, brick
And castaways made strange settings for animal
Life which managed to survive . . .
An occasional, misplaced deer
And single, gray, botched up and seemingly mangy
Fox ~ spotted once in a while. (I'm sure on a homicidal trek!)
And an unusually resilient colony of cats ~
Some living in a concrete, curbside drain,
Pestered by possum and raccoon ~
And the usual spectrum of rabbit, bird and squirrel . . .
All in all, not a particularly
Stellar group of tenants
Which one might place among the "great" of Yellowstone!

But it's all now a part of one place held dear
Which I see in terms of lavender
~ and with unconditional permanency, I hold
A forgiveness of its unkempt state.

I place that scene, preserved, encased
~ All its faults now but a small aside ~
To abide with nostalgic, love-connected thoughts . . .
Until the essence of my life and cherished field
Shall, together, someday rise and fade
As with its morning mist.

The Artist of Mesquites

Oh range mesquite, your swirling, ghost-like limbs
Have come to form a question mark when art
Has failed to grasp the daunting essence of your being . . .
Light green leaves always floating, so it seems
Within pale blue sky and billowed cloud
And, at night, your thin, gray leaves also rise
Like streams of smoke into a moonlit sky.

Tell me, sage, can one sculpt such an apparition ~
On with dabs and dashes of color paint
The haunting presence of that soul laid bare
Upon the prairie's rugged floor?

I stand now before the tiny, pale green forest
Spread light upon the rangeland grass
At once alluring and forbidding
And wait as with hat in hand
Before the mystic, elfin wood
For some fairy or select, enchanted leprechaun
To emerge and tell me just how I might construct
An artistic tribute to its magic habitat . . .
Or how I might render such lacy whisps of green
And ghost-like, curling forms of gray ~
Lighter than the air . . .

and loneliness is a part
Of its wind-driven boughs.

Upward Unto Mountain Pathways

C. Keyser

FEATURING —
"STREETSIDE" AND
SEVENTEEN OTHER
ORIGINAL POEMS

A Seed Once Planted

It was a mountain forest rangers' crew
Of which I was, then, so small a part
~ a dozen or so of us ~
Working in pairs
~ walking one behind the other ~
Seeding fir trees ~ sowing
Swaths of land in semi-straight
And mostly rough-laid rows.

The plantings took place through
Large plots of barren land
Of "burnouts" or "fallouts"
. . . any place erosion threatened
From a previous cutting of the forest growth
Or some type of random, natural cause.

One team member would walk
With measured pace
A few steps before the other,
Making single chips into the soil
With a type of heavy metal hoe.
The other wore an apron with its pocket full of seeds
Of which
Just five or six would fit inside the dipper;
An empty metal cartridge shell
Soldered to a short wire handle.

"Don't waste time by covering seeds once
Dropped inside," the crew chief said
"Nature will do that job for us!"
Then, in a prophetic sense, he seemed to speak,
"There is no way to tell just how many
May take root within the soil . . .
One of five, or ten, or twenty . . .
And of that group, a small percent
Will mature to sapling height."

Today ~ after fifty years ~ and
A thousand miles removed,
I wonder how many made it through
To full-grown towering trees.

But once in a while, I speculate
That timbers from those thousand seeds
Might form some part of homes
Or, one day, an historic edifice . . .
Perhaps some furniture, cabinet,
Ornate carving or picture frame . . .
Perhaps my casket plank or even
Pulp upon which this wooden pencil writes.
One tree will hold the wing which
Waves good-bye and the waving boughs
Of a thousand moonlit nights
Will also bid adieu to me.

Perhaps a squirrel from one such tree
Will view with curiosity
As some others ~ young enough to be
My grandchildren ~
Plant trees in just the way
As I once did.

And who knows? Perhaps
Some wayward seed ~ the
Most unlikely of them all ~
Might have grown into a noble tree
Which will look down upon
Man and other forest giants for
Generations yet to come . . . to shade
The lover's walk or to inspire
Some poet's dream . . .

Black Bear

Out of storied mountain haze
The black bear steps in front of me
~ as always, unexpectedly ~
Into legend's part of life,

And as a type of fable too,
He, again, will vanish soon
~ after one unexpressive glance ~
Back mid clouds and mist
Into a world of which we dream . . . one
Of unspoken myths and magic tales.

(A Conversation Between) An "Old Man" and the "Upstart"

Oh, my feet are set a dancin'
With the grandeur of my new and lofty
Rocky Mountain heights!
I'm "goin' to town" ~ goin' to "cut a rug"
On the ballroom of my prairie floor,
Spread wide across the spacious, western states.
Goin' to strut with my aspen-colored tux,
Decked out with golden studs from "Californie"
And silver mined right nearby
In the southwest of "Cola-ra-do"!

Ah, what splendor! I've outgrown
My Appalachian daddy ~
He's kinda turned into an old stodge ~ glarin'
At me across the "Missisip."
But I think he kinda admires my generation
Who now looks down upon his "pap."
Me,
Grown full-height now
Bedecked with the mightiest of trees
And highest mountain peaks ~ growin'
Right up through the clouds!

Why, I think I'll dance all night ~
Break into a free-form spin of sorts ~
Goin' to "jazz up" the bandstand with
Bob Wills and the Texas Playboy brass . . .
Throw in Gene Autry and Sons of the Pioneers
~ Maybe a shot of the Mormon Tabernacle Choir
Just to complement my dignity.
I'm gonna strut a new age "true rock" dance
Improvised and fresh!

"Not so fast, you young up-start!"
Comes the mighty Appalachian cry,
Hand me down my fiddle and bow!
I've got a few million years on you
   ... Sonny ... !
Gonna match you every way you turn, by gab!
Gonna chum out old Mac Wiseman
And his ageless bluegrass band ~
"High, blue and lonesome," honey.
Gonna dig me out some of those tobacce-spittin', banjar players.
Shoot that real down-home, foot-stompin' music to me, babe ~
"Wall-to-wall, tree-top-tall."
Think I'll freak out on a song called "Kentucky"!

The trouble with you young "upstarts" ~
Just recently shootin' up through the crust of earth ~
Ya got no respect for your "raisin-upins"
~ got no romance in your souls!
I'll take my dignified and rounded boulders anytime
To your brash and jagged peaks.

Think I'll doll up with my coal black suit
And Ozark pin tonight ...
Or dress up in my brilliant, Shenandoah best
And show you the *real* "Dark-town Strutter's Ball."
I'll meet you, kid, in Nashville!

Armadas

Mountain chains ~
As masted ships they seem to sail
Through ages past and those to come
~ These Armadas of the earth.

Mountain Bluebird

Oh tiny, mountain bluebird
How you've always chosen
The lovely and the best ~
As I wish, each day, could . . . .

With blue-gilded, feathered flight
You've embraced and climbed
To majestic, mountain grandeur,
And with heartbeat, flitting wing,
Touched the cloud and morning mist.

You've lit within the towering peaks
And through early mist have kissed
Both redbud tree and flowered vale.

Your image has bordered some
Of children's rooms, decor, and books
And artist's brush has captured,
Oft times, the wonder of your wing.

At last, it seems, you've somehow flown
Into the roofless chambers of my heart
And found eternal lodgment
Within its treasured, lofty heights.

Keyser, West V.A.

Oh namesake valley town, viewed only once
Through changing clouds of mountain mist,
How might both our lives have changed
Had they intertwined back then ~ transformed
From what has been and what now is
Within the haze of time and space?

Stranger ~ friend, I've yet to meet ~
Have you also thought so oft as I
What type of life you might have led
Within some random, once-seen place
Where answers still ~ though unfulfilled ~
Waft forever, good or ill,
And could have so easily been?

My valley town of lost reunions
Where remembrance lies unfound ~
And beauty unpartaken of . . .
What might these things have meant to me ~
A moon hung bright o'er Keyser's Ridge
Bathing features of another face
. . . so many miles and years away . . .
Names uncarved in oaken wood . . .
Beside me, steps untaken, whose
Hollow echo bespeaks a friend . . .
Or valley's wind a sweetheart's breath . . .

I stand before an open door
With shadowed yet familiar face.
Children play ~ among my own ~
Beyond the churchyard gate
And the gravesites yet intone
With tender thoughts . . . though n'er to be.

Oh, Valley town of Keyser, West V.A.
For me, empty now, except in loving thought
Of what might ~ and could have ~ been . . .

Falling

Loss of footing
Lost control
Falling
Falling
Falling
Helpless
In the void
Beyond the pale
Of what once was.
Confusion
Fright
Dependence
Upon the fate of stars.
Falling
A scream perhaps
Or just
The thrill
Of silent wonder
Falling
Falling
Falling
Once, too,
I fell in love . . .

Wolf Creek Pass

I shall pick up these random lines of verse
Where once I laid them down
Upon the treacherous, winding mountain road
Of Colorado's Wolf Creek Pass
. . . a drive where beauty once mixed with fear,
Years ago, along the narrow, steep incline . . .
Where guardrails seemed inadequate
And prayers were said for brakes to hold into
A serpentine decline down to Durango town.

From there, one thin strip of silver pavement
Ran its northward course halfway up
Other snowcapped mountainsides ~
Much like the tiny river/streams
Swerving too
Within its distant, canyon floors.

That beauty yet remains today
But within the safely broadened roads
~ Much like an empty lair of wolves ~
The ascent and incitement
Of my racing heart is gone.

Streetside

Don't delay, my friend, that lifetime trip
Which, like happiness,
Has always lain so close at hand.
Rather cancel tour guide plans
And leave your bank account intact.
Forget the waiting, pain and cramped suitcase
And join with me the grandest tour.

We shall embark this very hour
From your open doorway
Down the streetside way to mine
And your exercise will be a fond aside
To the rapture of awaiting scenes.

You may stroll or walk your chosen pace
And take whatever route you wish
While at your feet astounding vistas wait ~
Curbside gravel, sand and concrete shape ~ exotic
In both scope and form ~ endless designs ~
Small works of art ~ painted by the wand of God ~
Master sculpting fixed in deep relief
Upon an asphalt base.

There, strips of sand at once become
A thousand desert shapes ~
Shifting, changing, day-by-day.
And caravans may travel in your mind
Across its million swirling sands.

You shall also come to creviced plain
So exotic in its rugged form
As to rival South Dakota's Badlands
Or parched inroads to Devil's Den.

And if you will but permit yourself
The simple joy of thinking in

Dramatic scale,
Further, undreamed views of scenic wonder
Await each passing step . . .
Creviced pavement, wayside ruts and drainage ditch
Eclipse Grand Canyon's depths ~
Its wonder and its scope . . .
There, clods and stones of various shapes
And random mounds of earth
Will also dwarf Sierra's mountain heights
And pale its lofty grandeur.

And if you will allow yourself the luxury
To think in miniature,
All tiny pools and runs of water
Will transform into a thousand
Rivers, lakes and streams ~
Each with sandy beach or jagged, rocky coast.
Then, at certain times
When snowstorms turn to rain,
Across the streetside's flooded dale,
You may see a glacier slide from mounds of snow
And melt into the sea.

Perhaps, later, for a most exotic venue,
You might allow the million specks of gravel white
Within a blackened asphalt road
To signify the midnight stars of worlds unknown ~
Or bits of sand and pebbles rolling loose
Across the traveled way
May represent a distant universe
As yet unknown to man . . .

Just take one tiny stone within your hand
And realize as you turn it slowly ~ that fingerprint's
Unique ~ in all of time and space.
This ~ a planet ~ one thousand times as large
~ or a hundred times as small ~ as earth . . .

So far beyond the reach of telescope or travel
That its place will forever be unknown.

Still, within that eternal instant
Of all the circle bound in space,
Each has and will affect the other
In ways which we may never realize.
And if you will but let your thoughts take flight,
The surfaces of unimagined worlds so far beyond our own
That no hint of them will ere be known
May be cast upon your wayside path.

Stones the size of earth might be a common sight
Upon that billionth planet's crest
With valleys a thousand times as deep
As any known to us herein.
And mountains ~ oh the mountains ~
Rise a million times as high!

Wayside clumps of grass and edge of lawn
Will become some sort of exotic forest plant line
With trees a hundred miles in height
~ all those forever strange ~ unknown to human kind.
And even trash will play its part
Within the imaged banks
Of some distant cosmic scene.

Whether one looks upward to the stars
Or downward to the wayside scene
All wonders beckon much the same ~
And perhaps you will behold this glimpse with me
Along the concrete, sandy path . . .
Along your graveled, asphalt road.

Environmental

Do not build atop the mountains
Or crowd the river's edge
For one should be forever free
To paint, photograph and view
The unobstructed work of God.

The Appalachian Trail

Melancholy and forever's mist
Rise as past legions trek before me ~
All silent now, yet each one's story
Seems whispered still through forest leaves
Along the Appalachian Trail.

Seasons change and climates too
As time-bound travelers continue by
From Maine to Georgia
~ Two thousand miles ~ traversing fourteen states.
Traversing generations, too, like pages of a book.

As blue mist moves across the mountainsides,
Much like a hand touching here and there,
So, also, move those travelers too.
And mist will disappear from time-to-time
As the romance of its bygone lives.

Somehow it seems the souls of both
Earth and man's laid bare
Upon that trail worn sometimes deep
By moccasin and early settlers' feet ~
Each leaving there life's story told . . .
Some with grief ~ some with song.

I, too sat foot upon that upland path
In the sunrise of my youth
When fragrance of the mountain rose
Bled into morning mist and lungs.

And though, today, I view from mountain crest
I can but dimly see the end . . .
Futility couched in lovely grandeur
. . . Diversions, too, in colored robes . . .
As crystal, flowing mountain streams
Become a sedative to fate.

Now as my sunset part of day recedes
Into a moon and starlit mountain kiss
~ That blown gently by departing Breeze ~
I, too, shall leave my marker there
~ Among the rest for what it's been
My own legacy of life and love
. . . Upon the Appalachian Trail.

Mountain Goat

Amidst the beauty and the grandeur
Of Pacific Mountain chain ~
A land for highland monarchs
Where massive granite spires
Drive through cloudy rings and treeline
Into celestial blue of paradise ~
I see its shadow move undaunted
With unfettered, sure-foot confidence.

Though obscured, its form is majestic in that set
As the king of heights ascends unto his throne . . .
Yet what a paradox in contrast ~
This potbellied, spindle-legged goat!
Though always unapologetic, he clearly still does not belong
In realms with eagle, mountain lion and ram.

Still, up snow-capped trails he makes his way
Through upward, lashing, sea-swept winds,
With determination and reward known only to himself.
Click, clack, clatter, click
Tiny steps through danger ~ upward always to his goal
Until ~ among the pinnacles of earth ~
He steps atop the highest spire.

Then he seems to breathe a sigh ~
Bony, rib-sides only slightly moving ~
As steel-gray eyes look beyond a hundred miles
Almost, it seems, into eternity . . .

Though not human, I wish to ask him
Why he set the goal and made the climb?
And the only answer is what I surmise to be
A look of satisfied bemusement
With dispassionate chewing of his cud
And movement of goatee.

And if I could cast the unlikely little caricature
Into the form of humankind
I would further guess his life to be
One who earned his fortune crushing stone
And spent it on some great artwork
To treasure and to keep
~ thrilled with his reward ~
Though perhaps not fully understanding why.

Gratitude, "TToo," Begins With "T"

Even lightheartedly, the "TTwo" yet seem to merge ~
"Double "TT's" upon the field of play
. . . Texans and the Titans . . .
One begotten of the other.

It was also brought to mind just days ago
Off the main street of Gatlinburg ~
Lost behind the glitter and the glitz
. . . Historic contributory forerunners . . .
To the state of Texas ~ land
Which beckoned, too, as call of home.

Church of Christ and "Country Cookin" signs
Beside Texas flatland or hillside roads of Tennessee.
Also, both have "T's" of orange on white
For sake of academe.

And I hear music rising now
Like mist from mountainsides and western plains
. . . "The Tennessee Waltz" and "Waltz Across Texas". . .
Casting each its spell of love.

Country music's father, Jimmy Rodgers,
First recorded songs in Bristol, Tennessee.
Yet he played out his life with old T.B.
In his Kerrville, Texas home . . .
I guess he really meant it when he sang
"'T' for Texas and 'T' for Tennessee"!

Trail dust . . . I see it rising too,
Southwestward from the mountains ~
To the gilded walls of San Antone
Legends, Davy Crockett, Jim Bowie
And the host of volunteers
Shed blood upon and for that Texas shrine.

Sam Houston ~ he never tired
Until both states for which he served
Stood within the union fold.
Regarding him and all of those from other states
Who helped the star of Texas rise
Few, I suspect, would disagree ~
"Thanks," for sure, begins with "T"!

Hills

Hills ~ baby mountains ~ many
Yet unnamed and most, perhaps, Unknown,
Except to those who live nearby.
Still with each a wondrous beauty . . .
All distinctive ~ as fingerprints
Of angelic hosts.

Familiar hills ~ some not much more
Than nature's floral mounds ~
Become, within the essence of my life,
A type of altar reaching upward . . .
First to taste the blessed sun.
Last to see descending flame.

With silent gaze, they view the stature
Of how I've grown beside them
And for ages after I have passed,
A memorial to my life and love . . .
A reminder forever etched
To God and man on tabled hill
Of what I could and should have been . . .

Imaged Mount McKinley

Majestic Mount McKinley, crowned by Northern Lights,
Towering o'er the landscape of our lives ~
Of all continental mountains, glaciers and the sea ~
Upward unto thee it seems our better selves ascend
. . . always upward . . . past northern boundaries.
Then toward heights where moving sheets of ice
And changing mounds of snow transpose our thoughts
Into reminiscent dreams ~ changed, too, by mist and cloud ~
And helps us see far out ~ beyond ourselves . . .

Twin, matching spires of faith and hope
Looking over problematic lowlands
Buttressed by a golden core of love
Whose towering precipice stands always ~
A symbol of enduring strength.

May I always stand in awe of mountain grandeur.
And may the value of such humble, inner strength
Grace this surface cleansed by frozen rain
With a beauty known to God and man.
And may your own Mount McKinley also rise
With glorious dawn and Northern Lights.

Halo-cloud

Halo-clouded crown of mountain heights
~ Friend of heaven with feet of earth . . .

Mountain Echoes

"How lovely are the light green, budding mountainsides
Which come alive with blossoms in the spring
. . . bewitching . . . with fragrant breath and tender youth."
Those are among the last words I remember
Which you spoke to me at dawn.

Then I recall with summer's verdant green
How you touched my hand and stood amazed
At the panoramic scene ~ viewed sometimes, too,
From expansive bridge, stone mountain tunnel exits
And wide expressway cuts.

It was contagious, for I found myself enthralled
At your wonder and your words ~
Speaking of majestic mountain heights
And their lofty boughs of green.

"Magic" is the word so often used when
You spoke of fall . . . spellbinding, flaming
Colors torched by God.
And how God struck the rock also ~
From which living waters flow . . .
Lacy, intermittent streams, touched,
It seems, by guiding angel hands.

"Dazzling" is the word you often
Used when winter snows lay upon
The peaks and quietly spoke the mountain's
Final message unto man.

And now I fully realize
~ as everlasting ripples in a pond
How Mountain echoes speak those same reflective words
. . . So very true of you . . .
Resounding always back to me.

Upward

As I view the beauty of hillside heather
Fading upward into mountain mist,
I see the souls of its religious folk
Fade upward with it too . . .
Upward to the place where mist becomes a cloud
Yet upward still
To where mountain cloud has cleared . . .
Upward ~ even to ~
The lofty Source of Love . . .

May God bless you with His richest blessings,

J. Robert Keyser

The USA in verse

by J. Robert Keyser

16 ORIGINAL PATRIOTIC POEMS

FEATURING:
"POETIC DIVERSITY — ESSENCE OF OUR LAND"

What is a Song?

What is a song if not
Some treasured poem
Set to musical refrain?

Poetic Diversity ~ Essence of Our Land

PRELUDE:

Poetic shapes of earthen grandeur ~ each diffused
Through foliage into lace of air ~
Sighing, every one, its breath of life
Into and through an unfurled flag . . .
Just so, prose with verse ~ and that alone ~
Extols through flowing current winds
The song each region begs to sing.

Such storied anthems of our land
Have arisen thus with earthen breeze
And words carved from that flow
Become our nation's melodies ~
The expressions, true, of soil and selves

So I shall first extol prosaic verse
In this prologue to diversity
And pray that, from this day on,
I may not simply look but truly see
And celebrate its many parts.

From that air and dust must, too, arise
A people made of both
As back into its midst
They will also someday fade ~
Those who from its rooted plants have breathed
And from its earthen stores have fed ~
Are they, each, also not a portion,
Made of themselves for good or ill ~
Its product and its song?

Thus earthly elements, all of us,
Have one stanza's part
And the degree to which we
Complement our land of life

Is the gift back into its soul . . .
Unto the poem that we
Have made the strain eternal ring.

And in that great Eternal Instant
Which we falsely claim as time,
One ~ no matter what his station ~
Will not influence more or less
~ no matter who that one may be ~
Than the next within the ring.

The Devices, buildings, art and science
Drawn from those earth ties, too,
Portray the nation's essence in their songs ~
Each deed, each thought, each word
Tinged also with the lifeblood of its soil.
What we've built in earth or space ~ and
What is yet to be ~ reflect
Disparity within the land
From which our builders and designers come.
And our shopping malls, also elastic, communicate
What one or all combined say in metaphor
Of graven earth links to regions of our land.

So I shall exalt the builder in that respect
If he will not construct upon
~ and, thereby, desecrate ~
The place where God has left His print.
I see, too, the ends of all philosophy
As an evolution upward from the clays of man.

~Soils~

Soil, foundation floor of life ~
Bedrock and wellspring of diversity.
Each hue as vibrant and exciting
As the races, creeds, and colors drawn
From the soils of man and reflected thus

~ within our colors waving ~
All parts distinctive yet as one:

Have you truly seen the red soil of our land
At places where the earth's laid bare
And wonder at its
Cherry-tart and iron-rust earthen sea?

I stand captivated
At that red and rolling ocean scene
As enthralling as any sight upon this globe
And care not whether the soil is rich or poor . . .
Yet marvel that it contains such nutrients
As to make it grow plants like all the rest
. . . that such flaming beauty and functionality
Can be combined in one!

In matching beauty, upward from its midst
Will sometimes rise the red-tailed hawk ~
A shining poem, gathered, so it seems,
From Indian lore, languishing
In the breath of its red earth,
Reflected, too, somehow upon the soil
By white-gloved fox and raging bull ~
All together a melody and psalm.

Waking in the morning, I wonder
If that soil is but a dream.
Yet, stepping out, I see its vibrancy
And thrill once more
To sunshine glinting across the crimson tide . . .
And sometimes I reach down to crumble a portion of
This wonder of the world within my hands ~ just
To see that it is real!

Oh, I guess if it were my choice, I would
Have my casket placed within its hold
Just to know the scene above is always
Vibrant, fresh, alive and new.

I now trace the beauty of that red sea's earthen flow
To places where its epidermal boundaries lie
And earth mound waves break upon
A beach of crystal sand.

White sugar granules – almost like a miracle
Processed as if by angel hands
Lying, glistening by the water – somehow
Drawn from the magic storehouse of its depths.
A friend to barefoot running, romance and tranquility,
To imagination . . . strange how it can incline the heart!
To ecstasy . . . to greatness, power and to dreams.
Though sometimes not rich in nutrients,
It's so in raptured view
As I see diversity even there in varied hues
Whether lit by moon or illuminating sun.

From a fertile sandy loam, I hear that poem too,
Reaching upward as with green-leafed psalm
From rivers coursing deep within
Resounding through its oxygen –
The breath of variegated plants – rising
Into breeze and flag with its peculiar strain.

Then rising, too, as from the sand of Kitty Hawk
A matching owl or beach bird mounting upward
Into some instinctive dreamland path
Shared also by white, arctic wolf below,
Each as within its song of hope and faith.

Looking now into my face, my arms and hands,
I could probably find a hue to match that soil
And would hope this bit of verse
Would compliment and not detract
From a heritage of that sandy loam.

A different melody yet also rings . . . arising
With the color brown – rich

With thoughts of hearth, folkways, and of home,
Comfort in the storm, stability and joy.
From its midst a festival is borne
And its blossoms, leaves and berries come to shout, "Olay!"

Is there such a thing as an average miracle?
If so, then, perhaps this brown soil
~ because of its commonality ~
May be the greatest wonder of them all
. . . this marvel at my feet and pathway, glimpsed
Yet sadly . . . so seldom really seen at all . . .

There is within its hold, it seems, the power
Of grizzly bear and elk
As its earth-hue falcon drives into the sky,
Its talons grasping ties to all held dear.

I can almost savor, now, that taste of chocolate earth
. . . the blessings that it brings to me
And ask what I can give back into its realm
. . . until we, two, once more
Become a part ~ one of the other.

Now ebony lagoons beckon with their strength.
Or is it a romance of the night on ocean waves
Which earth's black soil conjures?
Spellbinding . . .
Throughout my childhood and now in later years ~
Each time I traverse those darkened pools
Sliced across by silver roadways . . .

Within this type of sanctity, the dark, wild turkey moves
From a valued page in history as does, too,
The matching black bear's magic form.
With glistening raven wings also rise
Historic negro spirituals set among
Contrasting cotton balls once pulled
By earth-hued, calloused hands.

There is a holiness innate within that soil –
An exuding reverence as in earthen symbol,
Of the black-bound Holy Writ –
Its lettered gold embellishing
The worth of cultivated fields
Whose black earth turns to face the sun.
Rich, too, the bloodline flow
Of oil and layered coal somewhere deep within,
Bringing also forth its type of life.

At length, this ink-black sea must also ebb
As with some sacred apparition
And we are left to wonder in its absence
From whence it came and if, indeed,
It should return to mesmerize again.

There yet remains one yellow ocean made of clay
And perhaps man first did come from such a sea.
It is ours to find within that honey-mustard soil
Room for the final race of man which also will
Compliment this land with its slice of diversity.

Sometimes, much like veins of gold, its peculiar streaks
Variegate and run across portions of our land
Until they pool in sections so exotic
That its texture and its hue become entwined
As with oriental strains of music rising beautifully
From our nation's ground with golden eagle wings.

How dull this realm would be if not
For the color yellow, even if observed – yet seldom –
In blowing dust and sometimes gummy clay or
Within banks and ledges here and there
Providing – though with ratified variety –
The uniqueness of its treasure set apart!

Now, both in sunrise and in sunset,
I see the nation's yellow puma stalk
With reflective eyes and glistening coat

Leaving perhaps only one distinctive track
For us to marvel at within its matching clay.

Now, the beauty of diversity lies not
In terms of soil and race alone
But in the color of some lover's hair
. . . of brown or blond, of black or red . . .
One and all a rhapsody
Inclining each beholder's eye.

And as every song of earth is lifted high,
The influence of its surroundings
Cannot be denied.
I hear a psalm put forth by each
Who travel, partake of, and reflect
The soil from which we come.

Regions...

Today the regions of this land's traversed
So readily by train, auto or plane.
But, as sailing ships once plied sea lanes
Fraught by ocean waves - sometimes
Scaling typhoon driven ocean billows -
So the prairie schooner coursed the frozen waves
Of earth with wheels instead of driving sails.
And through the turbulence, they
- as through great earthen storms -
Challenged lofty mountain heights!
Then, how often did sadly break
The bows of man-made ships of wood
So tender in the power of nature's strength.
And, thus a psalm is lifted up of stones -
The bare bones of the earth.

Their song is one of towering strength
- each chain a character all its own
Yet all crowned with latent power
These parts of earth not worn down by elements -
Standing firm in the wake of tune.

I listen to the tenor of their voice
And find that some among its folk
Have weathered, too, and rise above
~ through gusty storm and cloud ~
To savor and, in defiance, finally see
The now calm miracle of blue,
So close to sun and stars and moon
. . . Drawing near to the place of God.

Yet, I reach now into the valley floor
And deep inside the caverns and the jeweled caves
In search of this nation's character.
Somewhere its heart and soul is found
Among the stalagmites and stalactites
A million years in making.
Strength is drawn from pulsing heart,
From flowing, hidden streams and oil, veins
Of minerals and treasured, golden store.

No matter how upward thrust the mountains,
The source must always come from far within
That commitment and foundation core.
Like a country music band, the melody
Of each region's played upon a different instrument
Yet the rhythm comes from somewhere deep inside
As a throbbing base accompaniment.

Profound, that random glimpse inside
The anatomy of earth
From whence we all have come —
And a return back into it
Would seem to be our destiny.

The forest region's leafy arms reach upward
As do the people of that living palace
And I read there songs of woodland, human lives ~
Some etched with melancholy,
Some with joyous ecstasy, and some
With sorrowed pain.
The trees and bushes likewise strain
To live and breathe, encumbered as if by
Those things mankind, too, has come know.

And every forest plant is different ~
Each one a single part of that trillion squared.
As these fingerprints are upon the earth
So, also, is each of woodland's humankind unique ~
Solitary, with roots in differing soil.

So, within that wooded part of earth,
I celebrate all verdant hues of green.
Yet see the forest as one enduring swath
Within what the flag has come to mean;

The largest, oldest living things who've ever lived
~ breathing and exchanging breaths with man ~
Are each their own, whether sequoia, redwood, oak
Or willow wisp and flowering tree. All with differing
Bark, limb shape, leaf and color ~ everyone a unique
Song, resplendent in its life.

I've come upon some plazas in the course of time ~
Breathtaking in flat, expansive grandeur,
With just enough ~ perhaps a hint ~
Of tiny canyon crevices and muted plateau shapes
And placid water pools or fount
Such bring thoughts of plains land . . .
Oh, God, the wonder to behold!
~ every bit as striking as wooded mountain heights ~
I never fail to be entranced each awakened day
At the impassioned sweep God took

~ not just with hand, but with arm also ~
And showed the world, with one leveled stroke,
Sweeping power as far as human eye can see.
Do you tire of this, my friend? Not me.

Do not speak to me of boredom
If you consider that to be
This virgin, flattened canvass
With just the slightest elevated touch
Off to one corner perhaps . . . to accentuate
The spectacle of flowing grass
And the song it sings as placid
As one drop within a vast, undimpled pool.

Especially small, half deserted towns extol/enhance
The untold, vaunted worth of meadowland and field
~ of purity, simplicity, freedom, infinity and all
Those words which endear and stretch as far
As imagination will allow!
I do not have to look up to see the sky
But just across the prairie
To gaze into eternity,
Lying straight ahead in front of me.

If it were to be destroyed ~
This vast wonder of the world ~
Oh, what a tragic loss . . .
Oh, what a tragic loss!

If you wish to avoid the bayou,
My friend, steer clear
Of those fragrance isles ~ the
Mystery, intrigue, and euphoria
Innate within the glistening perfume
Bottled with alluring names . . .
And clothing ~ black lace and evening blue . . .
Jewelry and shells to grasp, compel and thrill

~ all seductive as the swampland shadows ~
Where evening is the time of choice
And it seems to last the whole day through.
Is it noonday, dawn, or dusk?
I cannot tell and do not care while
Entranced and held within its grip!
And who really wants the entirety of light
To shine and to define
And erase all mystery?
This wetland song would seem to ever rise
As the sounds of Mardi Gras within our nation's flag.

Not infrequently, I would take my flat-bottomed boat
And, with pole or paddle, wander through
Its uncharted isles and waterways
. . . at times . . .
Casting safeguards and caution to one side.
Around each corner there is
Something different and intriguing ~ perhaps
An alluring feel of danger . . .
And at times an oasis of risen land appears
Where rationale would seem to flirt
With surrounding, mystic scenes.

Oh, the titillation, the pitfalls and the pain
~ but wonderment and thrill . . . as that of love . . .
Its quicksand and its peril of unfathomed agony . . .
The danger and unpredictability ~
But, oh, the lure and compulsive thirst for ecstasy
. . . To grasp the sacred marshland jewel.
To ply the waters . . . eternal . . . undefiled
And as wandering as the searching soul.

I can no more refrain from entering
That wetland paradise
Than I can forbid the pull of love
Or ignore the scent of marshland rose.
And if you reject the swamp

Do not try to define or to exact
The perplexity of love.

Then, the transparent warmth of desert sunshine
. . . cleansing . . . as its bleaching air upon
Pale, yellowed stone and sand,
Unobstructed by varied living forms . . .
I can, at last, see free to
Untangle my mind ~ as nowhere else on earth ~
And to explore with uninhibited purity
The complicated depths of self and soul,
Unencumbered there beneath
The searching, searing light of reason!

The negative space of such contrasting land,
As in a painting, accentuates
The positive space of regions roundabout,
Delineating all configurations
With the peculiar traits of each,
Thus, drawing worth and beauty to itself.

And I see, here, within the desert scene,
Both a rarity and a jeweled case
Where life itself becomes
An oasis set apart and treasured.

Decay shall not encroach as much
With rot and ruin. And etched across
The arid strata of its heights, the
Grandfather clock of time,
Set with eons of yellow, purple, orange and red,
Tells the vaunted story.

Somehow it retains a hold on you
With an economy of words
And speaks into the desert sky
As with a mirage arising ~
A priceless note in nature's shorthand . . .

All things reduced to their essentials,
Roadrunners, cacti, and yucca plants . . .

That song will ageless ring within
The lives of those inside its realm
And shall become an equal part of beauty
With all other regions of our land
Renowned in unfurled flag.

Indeed, the nature of every region's psalm
Is bred into its fauna and its flora.
Even, it seems, the water sources,
Aquatic life, insects and birds reflect,
Embellish and portray each earthen song.

And every state hewn from this nation's realm
- from tropic zone to frosty north -
Breathes its sigh of seasons - its unique blend -
Into our banner's cloth.
These melodies played of this our land
Become, therefore, that emblematic strain -
A heart song in poetic verse.

And I hear the voices of its representatives,
Its poets, artists, singers and all those
Of a scientific bent, preachers and philosophers
Depict a heritage.

At the end, I must extol, again, in treasured verse
The wondrous range of selections - exceeded only
By the freedom here to choose.
Thus, do not cast derision upon
The object of another's love
No matter what the fancies held
Lest coercion rule instead of varied reason.
Brand, loved one, that truth within your mind
And stamp it on your heart.

Patriot:

An ardent proponent
    because of
An appreciation and
Affection for
    a given
State of being.

Highway View

Ships arriving and departing
Across a concrete sea ~
Tributaries running
Into the grand concourse.
~ There ~
Is typified a U.S. portrait
By wheels surging always forward.

Somewhere above that scene
I will choose to build my house
And view with fascination
The spectacle of human commerce
Within our youthful nation's push.

And I would sooner tire
Of all wonders of this world
Than the stories I imagine told
Of those inside each car and truck.
~ I choose ~
Within that wonderment of movement,
To glimpse those lives in passing ~
Concealed and yet as close as I may be
To knowing them and the enthrallment of
What each life's journey may unfold.

From time to time, I also join
And become a billionth part
Of those myriad and varied stories
Which I surmise within my heart and mind
. . . Untold legions . . .
Of flowing mysteries imaged always
From my intriguing highway view.

Our Flag

Some sort of patriot's song
In tones of blue and red and white
Waves toward me to captivate . . .
There is something about the way
That wind catches in the folds
And expands within my lungs
Beside a beating heart ~
Setting forth a cadence
Of valor, hope and liberty.
So what . . .
If I'm a sentimentalist.

Mosaic of States

With reverence, I remove, at times,
A mosaic of our several states
From within my treasured, mental vault
And with timid fingers take
Each jeweled shape, in turn,
From its placement there amid the rest.

Then I rotate, slowly, that shimmering state
Upward toward a source of light
As I would a 3-D, glistening stone.

Transparent, each color differs slightly
As from a prism's light-filled hue
And a melody from every one comes forth,
Drawn from the essence of its being
~ of its people, of its history, of its store ~

There is no greater or lesser tile
And each piece fills its space as none else could.
Then, the grout of union's strength
Binds the single, matchless piece
- unique within a world of art.

Exchange

I shall not exchange
The pain of skepticism
For the death
Of blind compliance.

Secret Place

There is one appealing secret place
That only you would know.
Oh, you might have spoken, to some, of it
But only you and that sacred scene
Will share its solace to your soul.

Some would view the site as "everyday"
~ Perhaps not meriting a great deal more
Than a casual, random glance along the road
. . . A window's view, countryside or city scene . . .
Still, to you, it's special ~
A place to reflect and be alone,
If but for a moment just in passing.

It matters not what scene ~ that hidden place ~
Its accolades or attention, drawn of men.
There is something of the view
Held within that brings you peace ~
A private bond between just two
That draws you to its heartfelt realm.

Citizens

Early spring:
~ Flowers ~
Fresh blooming.
~ Air ~
Clean and thin.
~ Steps ~
Light and lively.
~ Hearts ~
Lyrical and lilting.
~ Dreams ~
Each refreshing.
~ Then ~
A skunk . . .
~ Nose ~
Twitching with hope.
~ Eyes ~
Glancing about.
~ Ears ~
Hearing life's song.
~ Its mind ~
Devising plans.
~ Skunks ~
Enjoy spring too.

Tornado!

I saw it striking down from nowhere ~
Mindless, heartless ~ yet full of power
To destroy . . .
Indiscriminate to those who block its way.

People wonder at that terror yet
Do not perceive its source ~ that vengeful wind . . .
Surprise and stealth with no appeal to track or reason . . .
Ruining lives to prove no worthwhile point. I
Have known some folks like that.

So Early and So Late

I will have truly seen the green leafed tree
Only twice within my life ~
Once in infancy and early youth,
The other when that priceless view
Threatens forever to depart.

Why does man grow dull to common grandeur
. . . To life and beauty so profound
. . . To defy true recognition . . . now . . .
In the noontime of his life?

I will attempt in vain to grasp that moment
Here and now within this time ~
To stand in awe and TRULY look upon
A scene of nature's beauty
Or perhaps something man has done.

Yet realizing that I cannot appreciate
These things . . . just now at noon . . .
I fault myself.
Or is the blame to be laid
At the callous feet of all mankind
In the midday of his life?

(Remember how it was said at the start
Of Christ's earthly ministry that the
Finest wine was to always be
Received, first, in early sensitivity ~
As in the blush of youth . . .
To be equaled or surpassed only near the end?
At supper, then, how sweet and fresh
That wine, perhaps, did flow
Knowing it would be the last
Within this life He'd taste.)

Still it's said a "new birth" can occur;
When "former things are passed away,
Behold, all things are made new."
Yet I know that moment, washed and cleansed,
Shall also quickly fade with time.

So I try now to grasp the silver chalice
And drink for all it's worth . . .
To taste afresh the essence
Of this nation's bounty ~
Its light veined leaf and flowered vale
. . . Yet always unfulfilled . . .

I, then, must sadly wait for eve
When the precious scene
Is to be so shortly felt . . .
To grasp again ~ for a last, brief time ~
Its wonder and its worth.

America, the Changing

For some time, my dearest Miss America
I've meant to write this letter
~ Penned with confusion and in pain ~
As to how you've changed
Since I first fell in love with how you were
Back in that pageant of 1957.

But how can I ever communicate
My perplexity upon a tear-stained page
Using this confounded computer!
Why, I can't even get in touch with you
By an old-fashioned "letter to the editor"
Written by this human hand!
Now its "e mail," ".com," "on line," "twitter" or
Something else always "new and different"
If I ever want to express myself
To you in a literary way.
Why, just last Saturday I wrote a song for you
But by Sunday it was dated
By your wavering, peripheral events . . .

We can't even talk because your vocabulary
Is changing so much all of the time.
Just this past Monday I found that
You didn't have a traditional phone ~
Rather, one of those new pocket gizmos
With cameras, bells, computers and so many
Other gadgets that my head is swimming . . .

Guess I'm left back in the dust ~
Just the way it's always been when
Someone new has come your way.
Oh, I could change . . .
But I don't know how much difference
It would make for the long term . . .
I'd be driven crazy just trying to keep up

With you and the "jet set" or whatever
New phrase will replace that terminology.

In the past,
I was always so nice to you
But it seems as if your latest craze
Is an age which points out all of your faults.
Well, psychologists say
There are those who thrive
On detrimental abuse . . .
For reasons I cannot understand . . .

I see that several of your husbands
Have already died
Since we've gone our separate ways
And you've put them in mortuaries
- Your museums - with dates
And expressions frozen on their faces.
Infrequently, on some rainy days,
You may go there for a brief visits
But usually
You're too busy out dancing in the streets
With every new suitor who comes along!

I guess you've always been like that
Without my having faced reality.
Your older neighbors across the ocean sometimes
Resent you because of it.
"Rather fickle," they would say, "Maybe
When you get more mature . . ."

Dearest, I must admit
That some virtue does come with change,
With progress and with modishness
And I guess those neighbors overseas
Are jealous -
Just, to a degree, as I also am today.
But please understand - for your safety's sake -

That with your lack of patience
Can also come great harm
And, because of deepest love,
I must bring myself to say,
This fault could even lead
To catastrophe or death;

Sometimes, with the thrill of quickening change,
You could lose a visionary's soul ~
Of both foreseeing and preventing
Problems which may, in fact, affect your life.
I must repeat that,
In your haste and loss of foresight,
Vistas of your natural beauty which I once admired
Have been destroyed and you have fallen
To crime, drugs and illegal immigration
All because
You've failed to see ~ to predict and to project.
Your enemies and (just look at the U.N.) you've
Developed quite a few, are quick to understand
Your lack of patience has cost your trustworthiness.

While I'm at it . . .
(I've refrained, because of sensitivity,
to mention this before.)
Perhaps it's best that I should add . . .
Well . . . you're not as morally discrete
As once you were when first we met.
You seem to have kind of let yourself go.
Why, I remember when
We used to "go to church on Sunday."
I . . . well . . . .

Alright, I'll admit it ~
Something new and exciting has also
Appealed to me as I've watched
You move along the fast track
And leave me far behind.

But, remember, change does not
Always equate to progress or to virtue
And there remains some merit in
Your old love, tried and true . . .

Hurricane

Everything started with the sea, ya'know.
It says so right there in Genesis 1:2

But sometimes earth ~
The upstart infant of this ancient giant ~
Gets to feeling a little too big for its britches.

The sea lets baby earth go its
Egotistical and thankless way,
Without giving it the dignity of being noticed.

Except for times when she seemingly . . .
Almost as a casual afterthought . . .
Decides to give the self-willed novice
A contemptuous swat across the rump!

Return Home

I see within her features now
The passage of a thousand sunsets
Since the golden dawn of my departure
And
Waiting long for a wish come true –
The vow of my return.

Changed now . . . yet somehow changeless
She's speaking still to me
With a rush of faded river blue
And
From that rose-blush fount of youth –
A promise call, "manana."

Some things which I hold forever dear
. . . A relic or reminder here and there . . .
Form a lovely, lasting starburst
And
Today I shall return from foolish roads
Back to a type of heaven . . .
To that paradise of home.

The Lunar Date with U.S.A.

At just one pinpoint speck of demarcation
Within time's endless, streaming flow
~ Amidst a flowerbed of stars ~
The fabled "date of ages" once took place
Between our nation's flag and moon;
When human foot set first upon
That crest for aeons left unstirred.

Eternal hosts beheld the spectacle
Awaited by astronomers of old ~ That
Date thought of by ages fore and aft ~
And serenaded by timeless songs . . .
Romancing this ~ at once the goal
And object of man's affection.

Reunion

Quite unexpectedly a childhood sweetheart comes walking
Boldly yet lightly through the nostalgic haze of years.
She lingers in the brightness of
A vague yet somehow familiar scene
Which has, unbeknown, been harbored
In the maze of my remembrance.

Although her face is fresh and youthful,
There is no infatuation as before.
The words we speak are few. Perhaps
She holds a rose from a bygone time . . .
It has not wilted or turned with age . . .

She may slowly take some petals.
We both will watch in silent memory . . .
As they gently float and settle to the ground.

Although she steals away, she will reappear again
But always unexpectedly, boldly, yet lightly.

The Millenium Stone

I place my hand upon the stone in Central Park
And feel its vigilance of a thousand years
Yet of the millennium age to come
. . . that rock . . .
Perhaps the only thing within my view
To have once beheld the ancient jungle hereabouts
Where now abides this city with its commerce.
And I wonder what stark contrast
Will lie within its realm
The next thousand years to come . . .

That providential stone rests within a time zone
Placed just now at the epicenter of the world
Where soon comes forth the midnight hour . . .
I join that moment along with countless others
As the sounds and lights of celebration
Reverberate upon its rock facade
With the falling of the Times Square ball
So very close to where it stands.

Within that same U.S. Eastern time zone,
Fate shall converge again upon the rock
. . . bordering Manhattan's art museum site ~
Now the art capital of the world
Moved, of late, from Paris, France ~
Through Long Island's eastern shore . . . reflecting
Jackson Pollock's art and Whitman's verse . . .
And near that "fish's tail." I shall set my hand
To paint, record and write . . . the last and first
Of both art and verse to commemorate
The last millennium ~ and then the next . . .

There follows in the very shadow of that stone
~ The world's financial nucleus ~ and
Along that same time zone ~ the military center

Of earth's remaining super power,
The Pentagon.

At last, within that same time zone,
The launching pad and symbol
Of mankind's greatest quests,
The moon walk and his computer skills
. . . that also . . .
Shall I commemorate with brush and pen.

So, fittingly, I reflect, once more, upon
That midnight, Eastern U.S. time zone hour
Where destiny arrived
As sunset and sunrise again would glint
~ As never quite before ~
Against the surface of that stone.

The Fabric of Our Flag

Once I saw my favorite teacher
In tears
Leaving her art room about
Halfway through the class.
I heard that she and her sweetheart
Had broken up.
Yet she came back before the end
And helped me along with my painting
Though I'm sure
She didn't feel like it.

Today I see faces just like hers
~ Weaving responsibility and what is strong
Into the fabric of our flag.

I don't know the names of so many
Millions just like him ~
Dead tired but
Staying up late the night before
Income tax returns are due. He's
In danger of getting fired
For something that was not his fault.
His kids have gone to the dogs and
An unpaid bill's sky-high.
It would have been so easy
To have not reported that extra income.
Yet he lettered it
Into the space provided.

Would you consider him a hero for
That rather ordinary act of honesty? I say
His name along with countless others
Forms the stitching which holds
This flag and land together.

He's a garbageman – with not
Much more of a resumé than that.
Unshaven, with a fat belly, clothed
In an undershirt hanging over his belt . . .
Killing himself with cigarettes. He never
Had any hobbies or interests besides, I guess,
Drinking more than he should.

A girl he once dated before dropping
Out of school married a wealthy man
Who hired an accountant to figure out
How they could make more money.

To top it off, he will have died at forty-two
Of colon cancer.
Yet, just the other day,
I heard him cussing out a man
Who had killed a cat . . .
Some type of instinctive goodness
Which holds the flag together
With a million threads
In a million ways . . .

There is a woman nearby who,
By all popular physical accounts,
Is, well, just plain ugly . . .
Rejected by society in general and
For the most part, left alone.
How easy for her to hate and ridicule
. . . To trash those of a better fate . . . those
With lovers, mates and friends . . .
To view, on every hand, those not willing
To be seen in public with her.

Still, she once took it upon herself
To help preserve a greenbelt
– For future ages to see and to appreciate –
Thus, our Miss U.S.A. in perfect truth;

One of a million threads of beauty
That makes our flag
Unfurl with wondrous splendor.

Bind so many stitches just like these,
Gathered from the cities and the countryside,
And you shall see the grandeur
That truly makes our land and flag.

World of the Mind

PRELUDE:

There is a world to be explored within
The endless cosmos of our minds
. . . just out of reach of those
Who refuse to turn the key of knowledge
Or ignite the searching light of truth.
Yet, for those who do not fear or falter,
There awaits with timeless awe
That treasured journey ~ equaling and eclipsing ~
Whatever ventures one may take upon the earth
Or any science fiction tale of space.

The cost of such a trek is minimal
And, as I cast about for some loose change,
I find that the exploratory trip is mostly free
And will spare a multimillion dollar budget.

You may take this trip alone
If that fits your mental state or mood
Or you may travel with a like-minded group or
With that special friend.

And the discovery thrills that lay in store
Are so vast in number and diversity
As to stagger any effort to estimate
Their rapturous sight or sum.

Thus, within our fleshly senses,
The thrill and size of such a sphere
Is boundless to our understanding.
And we can never come to know
The entirety of its scope or power
~ this marvel . . .
This planet of the mind!

So, I shall make no vain effort or pretense
To depict even in vague dimensions
But simply make a futile gesture toward
Some areas you may see upon "that way";

WORLD OF THE MIND *(THE **ULTIMATE BATTLEFIELD**...)*

First, it's ours to gaze with unmatched awe
Upon the one authentic battlefield . . . the mind . . .
Or perhaps that forum would be better termed
The ultimate courtroom, coliseum or
Playing field meant to determine
One's philosophy of life.

My friend, there is but that one
Decisive field of human conflict . . .
Only one that matters and is meaningful.
It stands alone in primacy
And is unique in its legitimacy.
The priceless rule of reason is
All that, there, applies and
The fouls of intolerance and coercion
Must be always held at bay ~
Regardless of the cost to any person's faith,
Standards or set of values held.

Even love, hate or conviction always now embraced
Within each varied human heart
Must never overrule
By force those of some different view.
Otherwise that "victory" will be empty
And encase within a shell of shame
All who would enforce their concepts and beliefs
By violent act, by might or will.

Let us look then upon the priceless wonder
Of this only grand and brilliant battlefield
Where the logic of one's persuasion

Must stand alone against the white heat
Of another's view if it is
To be declared a victor by
The honest and objective ones
Of earth's judging multitudes.

And the implements of this warfare
Are as diverse as the components of the intellect itself
And the range of its battlefield's set only
By the vastness of all reasoned truth.

Next, its mine to walk with ecstasy *(KNOWLEDGE)*
The halls of mental knowledge
... Awestruck ...
With the profusion of its resource
... Boundless ...
Are its scopes of challenge, founts of wisdom
And its heroes.
I can thrill to all journeys with those who've made them
~ no matter what the mode of travel or of research ~
And their excitement and joy spills o'er to me.
Each step is one enlightened
And no experience is wasted in that plain.
I am free to accept all judgment
—with time and deliberation g'vn to each ~
And, perhaps, add my own into the mix.

I lay my hand into
This treasure of superfluity
And marvel with a thankful heart at those
Who've added some part ~ large or small ~
To whatever category I have chosen to indulge
... Ranging ...
From a life's vocation to
Some idle, wayside whim.

Within whatever forms the avenues may take
~ Whether books, computers, films or perhaps
Some way not yet reckoned ~
I shall find tools, materials and inspiration
To aid my own exploratory path
And would count it all joy and honor
If I could help even in some small way,
Travelers within that glorious realm.

To mine those banks of accumulated knowledge
Is a lifetime thrill which can only be embarked upon
And a billion computers cannot contain the data
. . . Wrapped up . . .
Within those endless paths of learning
. . . Expanding . . .
From eternal riddles of the universe
To spiritual infinity.

Then, too, creative corridors of the mind *(CREATIVITY)*
Lead a billion ways within
Each mental palace, waiting only
For one to enter there,
~ Thrilling ~
To investigative challenge.
~ Solving ~
The perplexities of time and matter.
~ Unveiling ~
Mysteries of the ages.
~ Showing forth ~
Endless latent power.
~ Transcending ~
The limits of all other life forms.
~ Exposing ~
Some spark divine
Lent to the human mind
By the God-breathed gift.

Oh, the rapturous joy of running wild and free
Through that enchanting mental world
Where I can create self-chosen paths
... Landscapes, seascapes, and cityscapes ...
All these fashioned with a turn of thought
Or transformed in a moment
With a change of mood.
There a paradise I shall make for both of us
~ a place of love, of beauty and of truth
As a heartfelt gift to you
... my fellow citizen and friend of earth.

Though ~ if even blind ~ I can see
Through an eyesight of the mind.
And though, within prisons made of steel,
I can create a world, my own.
No force on earth can quell
The incredible tool
... to create, to imagine and to dream ...
Vistas of beauty, of pleasure ~ or of pain ~
The grandeur of passion, of benevolence
~ or, perhaps, that of greed ~
Any virtue ~ any vice ~ may become a direction
... Chosen ...
To dwell in the psyche, heart and soul.
It's up to each to select the abode
... for good or ill ...
In which he will come to live.
And, at times, the vision shall evolve
Into a dimension we call time and matter.

Then frozen back into concept from change,
My being stands judged through cessation of life,
Forever in the way the mind
Has, at last, been turned ~
Either toward thinking inward, selfishly and dark
Or shining outward toward receptivity ...

Retaining all that heaven holds;
The entirety of love, the light of total knowledge
And, finally, the whole of aesthetic realm ~
Full appreciation in its perfect form.
Such rapture awaits all whose minds
~ frozen at death ~ remain outwardly turned,
Achieving forever the ultimate light,
Shown into this endless sphere . . .
That incomparable world of the mind!

Sameness

Love lost ~
Love found.

The pain ~
Of despair.

The meaning ~
Of joy.

Tears and burning ~
In throat and chest.

The rapture ~
Of another chance.

The dew ~
On a rose.

The touch ~
Of compassion.

That word ~
"Thank you."

The smile ~
Of a child.

The thrill ~
Of hope.

The dawning ~
Of day.

Such things ~
We all share . . .

The Instant

At that exact moment between the pitch of night
And morn's first flickering ray ~
In a roaring instant of trembling resolve ~
Day seems to catch its breath.

Within that moment of thundering silence
Just before the bird's first song,
The mingled scream of pain and joy
Precedes the slapping sound of birth.

With dusk, the futile surge of man
Will have strewn its hosts amid the stones
And God would then despair it seems
Of starting again with the coming dawn.

But somewhere within the night
A child's voice may be heard . . .
And day will compose itself again
With that thundering, silent gasp of hope!

Rainbow

A bow is born within
The mist of life and nature
Depicting variances of races, religions ~
Of nations and of personalities ~
With some blending here and there
Along the boundaries of each.
This shows in beautiful symmetry
How all peoples of the earth
Can coexist within that varied arc
. . . shaped with love to match our sphere.

The Perfect Language

I heard the perfect language spoken once
By a people who lived upon a dreamlike isle.
They saw a world as they would have it be
And created a language in just that style.

Oh, pessimistic friend, let me tell you,
It was a beautiful and powerful language.
(With careless abandon, they left out
The words for greed and lust and hate,
Words of envy and pretense.
Yet, as with skillful, little kitten feet,
That tongue has changed the lives of men.)

Yes, the language is difficult, but
In my stammering, halting way,
I managed to pick up a few expressions
. . . You can too.

It seems as if I can hear them yet . . .
Words, seemingly from the heart of God
And uttered through His lips!
I heard the perfect language spoken once
. . . When my child was very young.

Nameless Intermittent Stream

Somewhere within an average day
I noticed, as a scant aside,
The meandering semblance of a creek ~
At times
Not much more than a tiny scar ~
The mere shadow of a water course.
It seemed
Almost a type of afterthought
. . . a whispered understatement
From the lips of nature.

Along its shallow sides
Baby canyons dipped here and there
With tiny mounds for mountain heights
And scattered bush instead of forest grandeur
. . . all things there in jeweled miniature ~
Natural, treasured cameos . . .
Exquisite, gem-like pools and fish
Within what may pass as tropic space
And a "beach-front" turtle's home!

Shortly, its tiny course became
But a faint delineation ~
Just a bare suggested trace
As the impression of some vague footprint
Placed here and there within the soil
Before disappearing for a span
. . . then forever . . .
Within the face of earth and time.

Sadly, that culvert was
Seldom even recognized
. . . much less named . . .
As are the river giants
Flowing beneath majestic bridge.

Ordinary people like ourselves
Often pass unnoticed too
~ Though all equal in aesthetic worth ~
With each life upon this planet earth.

(Ordinary Street Lamp) of Kinship

Strange how the truth occurred to me
Concerning the similarity of man ~
Fittingly revealed within a light and place
As ordinary as all who here abide.

My walk that evening was the same
As the stroll of any average person . . .
Pausing for a time beneath a streetside light
As others around the globe are prone to do ~
Watching shadowed forms cast forth
From lifeless objects there
Beneath that glowing light ~
Suggesting images that another, too,
Might have so envisioned,
Allowing imagination to take flight,
Prompted by just such common things . . .

(A Necklace of the) Nations of the Earth

Awesome necklace of the world
Acclaimed for unmatched worth ~
Each part's a separate stone
Renowned for all its beauty
. . . one and all unique . . .
In history and in culture,
In religion, clime and race.
Each framed within a circle . . . none
More important than the rest.
Let every one its identity
And independence keep while
Conscious of its part within
That wondrous ring encompassing
The whole of human kind ~
Formed of compassion, of cooperation ~
Of liberty and of love.

Weeping Glacier

Glacial teardrops sadly flow
Down once ancient, sculpted cheeks
Into a warming sea ~ That edifice
Weeping now for all the parts
Of mother earth now lost . . .
Through extinction brought about
By that very one of all its parts
Most blessed and gifted in our sphere!

Weep now, white, shrinking glacial giant,
For polar bear and vanquished children
Of your once frozen castle home.
Cry hard for all the species
Now lost through change . . .
Of rivers, lakes ~ of sea and earth
From tropics to the plainsland,
From desert view to mountain heights.

Drowned in a flood of tears ~
Our nation's land held dear . . .
Mourn now for the death of life.
Cry for subjugated homes.

Weep also for the eye pollution
Caused by those who desecrate
River vistas and mountain views
And for loss of virgin, jeweled land
Once set aside for all to view.

Weep last and hardest, blue glacial eyes,
For those of us who cause it all.
And may our lesson learned be not too late:
That to destroy this environment
Is to bring destruction to ourselves . . .

The Time Has Come

A wisp of curling smoke fades still faintly upward
And my shotgun's barrel remains yet warm
As I toss two empty casings into a muddy, rain-filled rut
Where the blood of a fellow, feathered citizen
Mingles now slightly with the water's edge.

Eyes still open, the final twitch of life's now spent
And resignation's sown within a last instinctive gaze
As he looks upon my form ~ still intuitively afraid
But not fully understanding . . . then a fixation upon
Impending death supplanting as it will with all of us.

At last he fears no longer and the tiny heartbeat's stopped
As has the gasping, once air-filled lungs.
Then a silence signifying loss reigns within the void
Where a type of hope
And lively, rustling wing once stirred.

All of my life I've enjoyed the sport and there was a time
When it all made sense because
Of the practicality and, yes, necessity.
But now the time has come to set aside
All pretence besides that of a painful game.

Now it's plain to me that all things of earth
Become one type of living organism
As we occupy the selfsame space
And share our mutual fate.

Genealogy

~ Portraits ~
On the scale of time,
~ Waving ~
To me from the past.
~ Loving gestures ~
From ones I have not known.
~ Ancestors ~
Come with winsome smiles.
~ Happy ~
That we have chanced to meet
~ Once wondering ~
Who I will have become.
~ Wishing then the best also ~
For all future family ties.
~ I discover them ~
Here and there on yellowed page.
~ Or perhaps ~
On records or computer sites.
~ With some slight note ~
Of who they were . . .
~ To be kept always ~
In cherished files of kinship,
~ Those precious parts ~
Of family tree.

Philosophy

I strain every mental fiber
Now within the course
Of my capacity to learn ~
Bent to the end of
Understanding first that
Thing of most important meaning ~
The primacy of life's philosophy.

My friend, your first task is
Also that of mine ~ if
Your set of values are aligned
With what is truth and right.
And a step off the wrong direction
Can spell catastrophe and
A death of what your goals
Should be upon this earth.

Indeed, virtually everything is
Based upon philosophy ~ regarding still
All aspects of art and science,
Of religion and of law . . . You scour
Each slant of life to see, if in fact,
It's based upon the rock of truth.

Get it first and get it right.
This is my fond hope for you ~
And to those who test and try ~
To see if that path of reason
Leads toward the source of light.

Compassion

"Compassion" is a word penned by
The hand of God ~ defining
Him if
      . . . indeed . . .

He is to be defined at all.

Geography

Ageless borders that delineate are
Comprised of structured earth and waterways
. . . And each country is a face,
Features formed by flora, its peculiar
Peopled land and fauna.

Each section of earth's expansive breadth
Speaks in a different way ~
It's being shaped forever
With the earth-tool of geography.

Carved deeply through endless aeons of ice and snow
Or perhaps by some type of sun-baked hand within
Millenniums of stone or jungle growth,
Genetic strains abide ~ so deeply stained inside
Our fiber so as to never be removed.

And yet I marvel that within
Each land there are some who
Look up and understand
The topography of a boundless heaven ~
Teaching that we should always be
One in virtue, one in love!

A Poem for Success

Free enterprise and Socialism
Working hand-in-hand
Influenced by divinity
And the moral codes of man.

The Whirlaway Waltz

I yet see a sweet but ill kept promise
. . . of love defined . . .
The illusion of its sacred meaning -
Always just beyond the limits of my mind . . .
That definition of its mystic nature
Eluding, still,
Within my fervent heat of search
By verbal keys of mind and tongue.

All people of all nations have
Sought to first define and then embrace
That enchanted object . . .
Yet never ends -
The futile quest of spoken word,
Compulsive in its vain pursuit
. . . loves explanation . . .
To be captured - but only so it seems -
Someplace inside a vapor's vague and streaming form,
Against some distant mountain's crest - or perhaps
To be discerned within countless worlds of
Billowed grandeur beneath an airplane's wing . . .

I rush, but as for fool's gold, pursuing
My search for love's description,
Cutting through surrounding, misty forms
- But empty, once again, of essence -
As the romance of her promise
Transposes into a million parts.

My Quest remains as I grow old . . .
To clothe that form of love with words.
I sense inside the music of the wind
A dance meant to disclose.
Yet, so very near, the whisper
Never comes but whirls away
Within the music
Of that haunting waltz . . .

—SPACE— #7

COMPANION BOOK TO HALE-BOPP COMET TIME CAPSULE

FEATURING —
"NIGHT LAUNCH"
&
Over a dozen other poems
including the climactic
THE CONCEPT OF LOVE

John R. Keyser

(The First) Night Launch

Prologue

While contemplating the total message
And, simultaneously, each word independently
(As the essence of eternity is scripted across
The single sheet of diagrammatic concurrency
As a time line viewed all at once),
Holy Spirit eyes have always dwelt upon
Its eternal, ordained will:
Our cosmos which has been called into materialism
From an innumerable host of alternatives
That will always abide within their nonsolid states
Of dormant conceptual being.

Each word ~ besides having meaning
In and of itself ~
Gains further character
From the words before-and-aft
Then again
From other words before-and-aft those words
Until the sum of all acts upon every word
To bring forth the total meaning within each.

Thus ~ though following in an order ~
Each word is the same age as the next
And within each group of words
Each descriptive thought is as ageless as the next.

So within the first words of my verse is seen
This "Child of Morning's Sun,"
His shadowy form ~ and yet at once ~
The distinct image of his own offspring
A million years from then . . .

Night Launch

"Beware, hairy one. Watch out!" I cry
To the primate dreamer a million years ago.
"Cast now your eyes upon the ground where lie
The crude tools which you have made
To skin the hides, to protect your life,
To feed your family and your tribe!"

From the jungle's tangled growth
Glowers the eyes of beast and man,
Waiting to pounce upon the one
Whose mind and eye is not upon
Survival's daunting task.

Scornful eyes from his own tribe
Are often laid upon this long-armed man,
Whose brown back is bent within the searing heat
As callous fingers ~ scarred and bent ~
Struggle to bind survival's load.

"I saw him yesterday," sneered one villager,
"Beside the pool where we labored hard
To clear a cave for our sick and old. As
He paused to drink, I saw, reflected, his
Eyes alight within the shimmering scene
. . . where the image of the day moon
Played upon the water's face."

"That time is lost!" they all agreed
(With guttural growls which today
We could never understand
~ Beyond a primitive, hostile roar).

"That moment better spent!" they cried,
"For the soothing of our sick, or feeding of the poor."
"His adz was stolen too," said one,
"While he gawked in wonder at the scene
Reflected in the mirrored pool."

The community agreed,
"No useless waste of our time or might
On his plans and dreams for stars above
Though helpful he thinks
They, perhaps, may someday be!"

Within our moment, I yet beheld
That kindred one.
While still upon his knees,
He emits a snarling roar and savage glance,
Showing white fanged teeth as he,
With bowed head jerking in defiance,
Glances backward toward his tormentors.
Then quietly downward to his task
He continued . . . hands rustling in the dust.

Then something like an expression
Came upon that leathered face
With heavy brow and a scar
Where one eye had been.
(That eye having been lost in battle to one
Who had surprised him while beholding heaven's wonder.)
That look was some type of beginning
Of what today may be considered
The semblance of a smile . . .
The curling of his upper lip.

With his head still bent low
And cautious ears alert to those behind,
An old dusty eyebrow arched upward one last time
As he stole a final glance into the blue ~
The strange curl lingering yet upon his lip.

Then he moved busily here and there around the camp,
Stopping to do this or that in ways and for purposes
Which we have long forgot.
(He seemed, from all outward appearances, to be concentrating

On common tasks with all the rest,
When, in fact, his mind, in part, was somewhere else, beyond.)
Strange ~ this hulking, bulky form
Moving with a sidelong limp rather quickly
But with objective and motive clearly in mind.

If I were to have ventured into his space
. . . within time's diagram . . .
He might have tried to kill me with his ax
. . . if, by chance, we were to have met.

With caution preceding mortal combat
We would have beheld the strangeness of each other
Measuring one another from head-to-toe
In preparation for the deadly match.

Yet there would be something a little different
About this man from all the rest.
Imbedded far, it seems, into the scarred and fearsome face,
A spark of what would come to be known
~ with the development of thought and speech ~
As a trace of tolerance
That seemed to rise
With a type of curiosity combined with wonder and confusion.

. . . We would back away from one another
Never daring to turn our backs in the process.
He watched me recede into the brush
Without his having attacked me ~
Though he could have killed me
With one swift blow.

From my vantage point in time ~ safe and unseen by him ~
I observed the stooped body standing still
~ transfixed ~
Staring with that one eye
Into the grove where I had vanished,
That same quizzical half-smile

~ differing from all the others ~
Still upon his lips,
The ax hanging limply at his side.
I would continue to watch ~ until at length ~
He shuffled and turned away
Toward the practicalities of his camp.

And there was something about that limping walk
Though strange in all its ways
That suggested a kinship between us two ~
Though separated by so many graves
That no historian could bridge the chasm
By word or estimate of time.

He would mill around the camp
Doing all of those primitive things
In primitive ways
That primitive people did . . .
Few deeds of which I might understand
As to how they fit the purpose of his day.

In his demure, though,
And through the subtlety of his actions
. . . If one watched closely . . .
Could be detected an attitude
Somewhat different from the rest,
"Is this all that there is?"
His motions seemed to somehow suggest,
"Branch beds for the sick and rocks for the grave ~
Is this the only way to prepare
And is it alone, the best?"

"Not so many years ago," he mused,
"The fathers of those here today
Criticized old 'Log Float' for
His 'wasteful ways' spent lashing
And placing together with various techniques

A strange-looking thing which they would call,
For lack of a better word, (in translation) a 'boat.'"

Like these today, they mocked him saying,
"What good will that thing ever be?
Even if you set it out toward the sea
Needless deaths will occur ~
As has already happened
To White Feather, Buffalo Hide and, even worse,
To our own little Dove Foot . . .
Wrecked by waves, whirlpools and storm
Not to mention sea animals and currents . . .
Lives lost besides
Your time and ours
Spent upon such worthless junk
~ and why?!
You can not give us one good reason
Beyond some vague hope for dreamed-of progress.
When asked to justify the loss of life
And waste of resources on its behalf,
All you can say is,
Because the challenge stands
Before me . . . just because . . ."

Dusk had settled about the camp
When I saw him next ~ quietly moving about.
(By now, I could identify him
By his limp and familiar mannerisms.)
Stealthily, he crept into the outskirts
And up the sides of the highest of hills.

He had selected that bright night
Without, perhaps, knowing exactly why.
The moon and stars of a million kinds
Shedding forth a light almost as bright as day.

He would act alone if so he must
. . . I could see it within his purposeful stride . . .
As he walked up to the highest plateau
Where the chalk-white surface allowed one to see
Moonlit details as tiny as an ant.

At his side was not his ax
(This was a moment . . . almost holy to him . . .
Not a time for war but peace.)
Instead, some type of carefully blunted stick
Hung down from that arthritic hand.

Slowly he raised it up so that he could see
Lashed ever so carefully to its end
A prime portion of wild boar meat,
"I burned it slightly . . . The way I like it best."
He said almost to himself with a crude vocabulary
Interpreted with perfection by his heart,
"Maybe you are hungry and would like to take
. . . just a bite . . ."
With that, he lowered the missile
Once again down to his side,
Then swung it upward
With astonishing strength into the sky.

I could hardly believe the terrific force
With which that twirling stick ascended
Far into the darkened sky
. . . toward the planets.

No modem day Olympian could have matched
Its distance . . .
With hammer, javelin or disc,
Because it was launched not with just the strength
Of a cave man's arm
But with the power of unbridled conviction . . .
And hope that rose from deep within.

That first night launch
Was at a vertical trajectory . . . a few
Degrees off to the left . . .
Hey, a space program has to begin somewhere!

Shortly, the missile rattled down about
A hundred feet from its launching point.
No modem day scientist could match with
Emotion or speed . . .
That limping run toward the
Point of touchdown.
Picking it up, he carefully studied
Both meat and stick
With an intensity from his single eye
That emulates
The enthusiasm of our modem scientists,
"Not a bite . . . Not a single tooth mark,"
He grudgingly surmised
After inspecting the complete payload.

Dejectedly, he lowered the missile to his side
And trudged slowly back toward the camp . . .
"I'll try again at the next full moon," he said,
"Maybe God will be hungry enough then
To accept my gift . . .
Maybe . . . just maybe . . .
He will let me peek and understand!"

Memory now grows dim of that imaginary night
As departing, I view his figure standing yet
Looking through the moon-lit branches
Stirred only by a lifting bird
. . . Wondering . . . in his own peculiar way . . .
I see him glance behind himself
- and to the right and left -
Then, with a degree of embarrassment
- or the forerunner of that human trait -

He did something which I shall n'er forget.
Lifting high his hairy arms, he waved them
Up and down as fast and powerfully
As he could hope to do . . . glancing downward
To see if he had upward moved,
If but an inch or two!
Then, with that bemusement yet upon his face
He watched the night bird upward wing its way
. . . as toward the moon and stars.

Death had not come
As an unexpected thing
Neither was he ill prepared . . .
This Child of Morning's Sun.

Laying, moments before his death
Looking up into the autumn sky
. . . quiet and still . . .
The soles of his leathered feet
Facing outward, scarred and worn
. . . no motion . . .
Except the blinking of his eye
. . . once . . .
And the nail of his right forefinger
. . . from a gnarled hand resting at his side . . .
Scratched lightly, but only once,
Into the loosened sand.
But what that single eye beheld
. . . no one except that one could know.
No remorse was felt by him.
As all astronauts to come
. . . he had to die of something . . .

Somehow, perhaps, he sensed that he was on
The same page of time ~ just in a different place ~
As those of future ages who were
To fly ~ yes, inhabit those expanses ~

Not for the good of themselves
But for the descendants also
Of those who ridiculed and laughed.

"Clatter, clatter, clatter" . . .
Stones, at length, fell down upon
The deep pit grave of this one . . .
The Child of Morning's Sun.
"Even this misled portion of us all
Will be spared from the fangs of hungry animals!"
They disparagingly cried, as the last protective stones
Were thrown down upon his lifeless form.
In truth, his type was building upward
. . . stone-by-stone ~ generation-by-generation. . .
As a way to save that greater portion
From the deadly consequences
. . . of its downward gaze.

"Good riddance," spoke one
As the last stone fell upon the wayside grave,
"Now back to those important matters
Of a practical sort."

Only one, Little Dove Foot's daughter
Took any time to ponder . . .
And that not long ~ only an instant ~
As she glanced once at the grave
Then quickly upward into the cloudy sky
With a type of questioning look upon her face.

Did she somehow sense, the same as him,
An intuitive thought, not folly then defined
. . . yet a premonition of commerce in the sky?

Postscript:

As I look upon the scene,
The falsity of elements which we term time and distance
Converge from the abyss of this caveman's space
Into the spectrum of timeless reality
Where upon the broad plain
Of diagrammatic concurrency . . . an eternal instant . . .
Abides all ages now at once - separated
Only by his veil of moonlit nights.

A Planet's Title

A planet's name once given
Seems to have built
A life of sorts
Into a lifeless form.

Though uninhabitable
And never visited
. . . a name . . .
Though figurative and just
A symbolic and empty gesture,
Will leave a type of "footprint"
Upon a place defined
By man, at last.

Transcending

Earth ~ slowly spinning
As it revolves
Into days and hours and years.
See it from afar ~ large, light green swaths
With streaks of darker green and tan
Dividing the waters beneath white
Streaks of clouds in movement also . . .

Astounding ~ the history of man upon
A globe, rotating, it seems to me, always
With an aura of profundity. The
Inspired acts of inspired humankind
Transcending natural law ~ a miracle it seems ~
Rising above earth's gravitation,
Somehow ~ through sheer will power ~ having
Loosed themselves from its very hold.

Dreams and hopes elevated by some type of
Spark divine ~ ascending ~ with sometimes
Lack of courage ~ yet grasping always
Forward, upward toward utopia . . .

Space Interrogative

My conversation would begin with a question
Which I may never have
The intelligence to ask.

Alone

Alone,
Alone,
Alone

        Forget the law of averages
        And statistics
        Respect the world's environment
        And each form of life,
        For this might just well be
        Simply all there is . . .

            ~ RIGHT HERE ~

The deeper my view
Through the hell of space
. . . through planetary, telescopic lens . . .
The more wondrous
The flowing springs of earth
. . . its flora and its fauna!

        Our Philosophy, art and science
        ~ The concept of love and searching
        For the heart and mind of God
        May be all the universe
        Has ever come to be

    ~ UNIQUE ~

And all the best
Within the total cosmos
Could just well be only
That which we now are
And will have become.

           ~ ALL ~

        Within this blue/white marbled ball
        With flecks of green exchanging life.

            After all,
            We are,
            Perhaps,
            Alone . . .

Infinity

Man pricks the outer rim of infinity
With his machines
And, after all of his great effort . . .
He, with less than the mind of a cosmic ant,
To contemplate the cosmos . . .
Might just have been going the wrong way
All the while.

"The True Super Bowl"

(Ultimate Game and Test of Will)

I fear, this day, that I must relegate
My vision to the written word
Since man will not arise
From the stupor of his ways
And let his better aspirations
Take flight unto the stars.

Yet I can plead this once
For a cause all people should support
Had we but the foresight and the will . . .

To comprehend this message and its plea,
For a moment of this reading,
Look not upon yourself or upon earth's pressing needs
Which, for the moment, cry to you.
Look not upon the night – the concerns even
Of death and health related things.
Think not of entertainment and perhaps the need it fills
Or time and money spent – no matter what the sum –
On matters of the heart or mind
Which fill your needs and wants.

But glance just briefly once beyond
The horizon line in front of you
– Beyond its crested shape, into the blue –
And contemplate long and seriously
The possibility . . . oh, the possibility . . .
Of one great goal accomplished
For all combined . . . and yet for you!

An earth of mistaken folk
If you will not coordinate
And contribute . . . something . . .

For each his own
Toward one single earth-wide goal
To which one and all contribute
. . . something . . .
For which all can feel
. . . a part . . .
Accolades from a million generations
. . . offspring of our own . . . if we succeed!
Condemnation from silenced, eternal persons
. . . lost, unborn generations . . . forever crying
If we fail to act as one.

Listen, mistaken masses, if you,
As in the past, fail to move as one on earth.
And only as a single unit can you succeed!
Take heed, for the chance is now before you
~ all of you now still alive.
And if any one of you fails to seize this moment,
Reproach of the ages will fall on you ~
A silent judgment which may not be felt
~ nevertheless ~
That which shall abide upon your head forever.

The goal is, in a sense, simple
~ one in which all people can and should participate ~
Yet so profound that perhaps no mind can comprehend
The magnitude of its blessed greatness.

Do it now or lose the chance
Forever ~ and for all mankind ~
Do it now, pray God!
The •objective is a simple one
As well as the •recipe for such
And the •results eternally profound:

For all people of this earth ~ for all governments combined:
The •objective is to send, at least, a person-kind
To the nearest star where it may live,

Using that as a stepping stone to other planets
Of this universe and beyond . . . for you and
For all mankind . . .
The •recipe is a simple one which
Must be followed with immediacy . . .
Choose a large place on earth with natural boundaries
~ large enough to accomplish the task at hand.
Say, for example, the Sinai Peninsula,
A place of transformation . . .

Next ~ the team of destiny,
A team of all-time greatness . . .
~ beyond compare ~
This would be a "Super Bowl"
But eclipsing all others combined and ever played:

Upon this field would be assembled 700
Of the richest now on earth. Each would
Put upon a large score board the amount that
He or she, through total sacrifice, will give.
The "referees" will tally on
The score board as each amount is drawn
From banks and posted to the applause
Of all ~ who would have cheered the athlete
For his sacrifice and prowess.
This is not all . . .
The "fans," 700,000 strong,
Will fill the stadium and pay double
What the cost would have been ~ for
THEY now have become a part of the
Greatest team assembled
Their names emblazoned forever on micro chips
Within the "Explorer's Hall of Fame" and
Tickets left to frame for posterity.

Each of 7 continents will have its arena,
Modeled just the same ~ as some soccer field ~ or
After another sport ~ it matters not.

The 7 amounts will be combined
As down payment for the secluded land ~
And then the challenge will begin;
Within each continent, within each village
Each and every person, rich or poor, must give something.

If just a penny ~ a type of census ~ missing no one!
Call this a tax levied by each
Country if you wish.
~ beyond this ~
Each free will gift will be tallied and an
"Ultimate Sportsman" receipt given
For one's trophy for all time!
Just for example; In the most impoverished land,
A goat may be sold for 1 dollar to play for a
Family of 5. This would be a great gift for
They have given from their need . . .
They have paid their part!

All who give have become as winners
And one can check the record book to prove it.
The losers are the ones who refuse to give
And let down the final effort with its final victory.

Now take that amount and give it
To the mutual cause, for the land, the scientific
Formulation team, the contract (constitution of sorts)
Drawn up, the buildings, the team made up of
All races and the supporting team of "fans"
Who weather the elements to sacrifice and
Stay informed via the printed word to find
What their team is doing, the advances and
Perhaps, the setbacks now and then.

They shall wear with pride always
The emblem of our team . . .
The one that really matters
Because ~ in it ~ everybody wins!

Keep the jackets, imaged flags, ticket stubs, etc.
Revere and pass them down from your generation as
One would cede coveted mementos from
Historic groups afore ~ even all the more.

I shall not tax you further
With details of this eternal, gilded team
Lest I grow short of space ~ and you of patience.
Suffice it just to say, the object's always clear . . .
Stepping stones in time and space ~ colonizing the moon,
Perhaps, as just a starting place.

Manned flights might achieve that end or
Perhaps, first, the use of robots or machines . . .
Maybe cloning or the use of half man /
Half machine with the interchange of parts.
What about a programmed robot machine with
Ethics and discretionary capabilities ~ and the
Capacity to reproduce itself?
I see, perhaps, another phase . . .
A programmed, synthetic counterpart
Flying faster than the speed of light ~
Dispersed with energy particles of that being,
Only to be consolidated upon its arrival at
Some cosmic destination . . .

No matter what your sense of this
Meandering verse ~ if so its deemed ~
YOU HAVE NO CHOICE.
You MUST be on one team or the other
. . . to participate or not . . .
To either win or fail
~ Right now ~
Which will it be?
~ You MUST ~
Answer to the voice of destiny,
ONE WAY or the OTHER . . .

O. K., reader friend, I can visualize,
Just now, the corners of your mouth
Turned up in ridiculed bemusement.
The above lines having been written
By a lunatic or witless dreamer.
But let me tell you well . . .

10,000 years from now, no one will CARE
Who won your Super Bowl, Olympic feats or even
Tests of will on battlefields.
But IF this game of which I speak
Were to have been somehow played and won,
UNTOLD GENERATIONS WILL RETURN UPON
THE STEPPING STONES OF STARS
TO SEARCH THAT HALL OF RECORDS FOR YOUR
NAME
WRITTEN HERE ON EARTH.

The Heavens

~ Cosmos ~
Perceived sometimes as dormant tranquility
When viewed from afar.
But . . . astoundingly . . .
Up close, the opposite
May be true . . . motion . . .
Beyond our wildest imagination!

Space Knowledge

Looking back upon
A time when I imagined ~
Almost as thrilling, then,
As to have really known.

Life Star

Astronomers, once gazed
Without the means of telescopic lens
Into the heavens, as we today.
Yet they, too, may have surmised
The secrets held within that view ~
A past life reflection within a multitude of stars ~
Flooding, still, toward the human eye.

One star among all others,
Now beheld and viewed, perhaps,
By those of old
In the eastern Galilean sky
Holds all the mysteries that it has seen
~ and, perhaps, even ~
The source of life itself.

My God is Proved Within Itself

I wilt before the spectacle of space,
Bewildered by what enacting force
Ordains and drives eternal cause.

I exude with rapturous awe
The author of infinity
Which proves within itself
All that needs be proved
To say it's deity!

(The Concept of) Love

I shall conclude these seven books of verse
With a poem formed in the eternal void
Of nonmaterial conceptualism
. . . written for all who claim to search –
Whether Moslem, Christian, Jew, Hindu,
Atheist, agnostic – no matter what the faith . . .
For all of those who dream, who wish,
Believe and hope . . . all of us . . .

Yet, I wonder if most really want to know
From whence God might have come and who He really is
. . . as all of the above profess . . .
Lest they would have taken time midst busy lives
To read the Eternal Instant composite theory in which
I've attempted to answer all those profound things . . .

Thus, perhaps as an empty gesture – unheeded by man
Yet somehow meaningful to myself –
I shall end this series with a poem
Depicting the fact that God exists and
That by the only truthful sight
– through reasoned truth of philosophy –
Upon which all disciplines are based . . .

THE CONCEPT OF LOVE

Space – jeweled thief of reckoning –
I have saved you last for contemplation!
Within the maximum security of your hold
The riddle of life is forever kept from finite minds.
So, I approach my quest for understanding with
The only tool I have, philosophy . . .

Within your realm is forever held
The eternal pain of perplexity
And, yet, the titillation of what we've labeled discovery.

We desire the quest for answers somehow to end
Yet hope and trust it never shall . . .
Always, at last, we're left
With some sort of faith
While battling with less than a pinpoint
Against the colossus of your eternal sword.
So, driven by our frail and futile brains,
We know, in this material state,
The quest shall never end.

The mind-boggling nature of what's been labeled
~ perhaps wrongly ~ time and space is always there.
And is my concept of an Eternal Instant true?
That, too, remains unknown.

Oh, space, eternal birthing place
Of beauty and of hell ~
Is not one the angel of the other ?

I contemplate with awe your endless magnitude
And with speechless wonder gaze upon
Countless cruel, hypnotic monoliths.
An eternal, screaming panorama there unfolds
With vast, lifeless spheres so eternal cold
As to freeze matter, mind and soul.

Then when one thinks of cold ~ as cold can ever be ~
Even that hell is intensified
By contrast beyond the word extreme;
By fiery globes so large as to envelop
Earth a billion, trillion times . . .
Where white-hot melted lava's flow
Cascades into endless lakes
Of ocean flame and molten white.

Then, empty, spacial reaches span
With more blackness
Than a quadrillion, decillion light years ~

Squared – then squared countless times again – forever beyond
The grasp of any computer or reckoning of the human mind.
– A state which suffocates despair
Within a nightfall of boundless death!
Where disorientation brings forth the fact
That mortal brain has never
Known its way at all.
Even earth's most insensitive mind
Will stand aghast
At this satanic, blackened scene . . .
More **terrible that darkness**
Than **the hell of fire and ice.**

I am **mocked by the quiet beauty**
Of evening stars and moon
. . . tales of love and songs and all related things . . .
Stroked and soothed by season's blush,
Sunset and colored dawn . . .

All these things in literature and art
Shall vanish at death without a final consolation.
The mirage of things important to the human brain –
All poetry, all relatives and human ties,
All world events, all lectures and all sermons,
All laws, governments, personalities and the devices of man
Shall vanish in an instant.
Enough of the "space alien" speculation!
Lost in that endless abyss, they, too, would be,
Hopeless despondency would become our mutual fate.

What, then, on earth was viewed as beauty
Would be **seen at death** . . .
As the awe **of hell forever.**

That which **was my earthly birth**
Is now but some type of dimmed impression

And the ending – an intuition . . .
The first, a matchless thrill of anticipation
And gradual dependency as I came into this world with hope,
Grasping for salvation.
The return will be so rapid as to make
The head of any mortal swim . . .

I perceive my soul and yours, departing faster
Than within a pneumatic tube
Into a timeless dimension –
That exit so out of control as to become
The action of an involuntary muscle . . .
Into a type of instantaneous flight beyond
The speed of light back into a sphere
Where time stands still – always –
Where there is no time . . .
This would be eternity . . . a fixed state.

Weightless, then, and hopeless, I waft
And rue with total helplessness,
My pitiful earthly ego frozen there at death
– stacked against the horror of reality –
Of eternal, endless despair and despondency . . .
Drifting, writhing, churning . . . my weightless being
– ever convulsing – turning without direction or control
In a state where all is meaningless.

Spellbound with eternal, horrific wonder
Within that ultimate loneliness of space,
I am now and will always be
Infinitesimal in its measureless
Hell-red lava flow and gargantuan
White explosions . . . each larger . . .
Than the melted brimstone of a trillion suns.

Thus immersed with overwhelming, speechless awe,
I am staggered in perpetuity by monolithic
Spheres so eternal cold as to freeze

Imagination and even the past memory of life.
And, even if a type of tear should fall
Through space upon the hateful, molten lava,
Though fried, would dissipate and disappear
Or fall upon a sphere so cold
As to dry-freeze and forever vanish.

But, oh, the eternal blackness of space
~ death's "shadowed vale" as spoken of ~
Blacker than the blackest black.
Smothering confusion, is that worse and endless state.

Perplexed with such immensity
~ despairing and despondent ~ in that hopeless void,
There is nothing left to grasp or place to turn
Except to surrounding lifeless forms ~ unfeeling and
Uncaring ~ as the cold and staring eye of death.

With almost loss of hope,
I grasp for anything to pull me from
The throes of deceit's eternal death.
With futility, I grasp for anything to seize ~
To deliver me from this despondency . . .
Anything to contrast . . . to somehow save myself
From the beast of that eternal, darkened state of space.

Then I sense, though faintly, a single, last and desperate hope,
Encased within despair eternal.
. . . Lightly . . . almost as a mirage at first,
I see a wisp of smoke ~ yet it is not smoke
Because a concept, weightless, cannot be seen.
Yet that thin, transparent strand is all that seems
To stand apart and somehow drift
Above the hopeless scene!
~ That Holy Spirit transparent wisp ~
Oh, rapturous instant of realization, it is all
That I can hope for or imagine!

~ and somehow the sense is mine ~ that I might even somehow
Bridge the massive reach of space upon that apparition.
I approach spontaneously yet with timidity, helpless
As once I was when brought into this world
~ Realizing ~ that I cannot enjoin except as a tiny part
Of that God which I revere and praise within this song

I will then attempt to grasp the priceless staff,
The eternal ~ concept of love ~
Allowing all who follow God the feast in heaven's realm:
• The thrill of boundless love,
• Total expansion of the mind
• And a full aesthetic sense.
And to escape the choking darkness of selfish, inward looking,
Is itself a type of heaven's blessing.

What, too, is judgment but a revelation
Of the state which I have forever chosen ~
My conceptual counterpart, my soul, always there
. . . awaiting for its fading back within . . .
Having always borne my departure and ascendancy.

Timeless Holy Spirit conceptuality,
I must now and forever place my all in you
When this sphere I leave for "outer space" . . .
Knowing the transparent concept of love
Is forever nonmaterial yet real ~
Wafting for me somehow to grasp
If I will have but forever done so.
Upon that flow, I loose, then, in finality,
The horror grip of fear
And lay hold upon the ageless, flowing train
Of perfect consolation ~
To rest always within God's paradise
. . . within that concept of eternal love . . .

Additional Works

THE GOLDEN KEY

The RANDOM STONE

The Golden Key

From prison walls of sin
He has released me.
I hear a welcome
Call for me ~
There, placed within
My thankful heart,
Is placed
The golden key!

The golden key of grace
Has now released me
From a grave of sin
I've been set free!

I am free to face a
New tomorrow ~ with
The gracious, golden key!

With the golden key of grace
He has released me
From the tomb of death
And sin I've come . . .

With the promise of that
New horizon, he has
Set me free.
From the hand of grace
I've been given
The priceless golden key!

The Random Stone (Named "Hildegard")

Just by chance, this reality
Came to mind – during
An unplanned walk afield:
There, upon the rock-strewn scene
Was a profound truth, seldom
Phantomed by the human brain . . .
For <u>miles</u> below our traveled paths
Lay <u>trillions</u> of unseen stones
Never to be viewed as these –
In the <u>light of blessed day</u>!

Now <u>every</u> stone is <u>different</u>
In its own peculiar way
And not a single one
Will a <u>duplicate display</u>!

I reached **down to grasp,**
Just then, the "<u>random stone</u>" –
Perhaps untouched before
By human hand.

O.K., I named that stone;
"Hildegard."
It didn't seem to mind
As it stared right back at me.

That tiny rock was unique
As all the others were.
Yet there was a common message
Calling from that stone to me . . .

"I can be your 'Rock of Ages'
Just as you may wish
For me to always be.

I will stick close by
To give you strength beyond
This day and
Through eternity!

You may, figuratively, 'lean
On me' as you do upon
That <u>true</u> 'rock of ages'
Throughout infinity!"

About the Author

John Robert "Bob" Keyser was born in the small town of Bryson, Texas but spent most of his childhood in Fort Worth. He majored in forestry at Fort Lewis College and transferred to Abilene Christian College (now University) to study art.

After graduation, Bob married his wife, Joyce, and moved to Aquebogue, New York to help with church mission work. They lived there for forty-three years, working full-time in ministry and teaching teen and adult Bible classes. He taught art at Riverhead High School for thirty-three of those years and also served as the district-wide art coordinator. In addition to regular classes, he taught adult art education and summer gifted and talented courses. In 1972, he earned his master's degree in art from Long Island University – Southampton.

Partway into retirement, Bob and Joyce moved to Sevierville, Tennessee for twelve years. They currently live in Wolfforth, Texas and have two children and four grandchildren. He currently spends his time making artwork, writing, going on walks in the neighborhood, and enjoying visits from his family.

Bob has written numerous works, including poems, short stories, children's books, and religious philosophy, alongside his many paintings and sculptures. Visit his website at worksofjohnrkeyser.com for more information about his writings, art, and exhibits/lectures.

Made in the USA
Coppell, TX
20 January 2026

68045412R00132